Fully Expressed Living

50 Perspectives from Stuck to Fulfilled

By

Jenifer Novak Landers

Great Little Book Publishing, Inc.

Sacramento, CA

www.greatlittlebook.com

Great Little Book Publishing Co., Inc.
Sacramento, CA

Fully Expressed Living: 50 Perspectives from Stuck to Fulfilled
by Jenifer Novak Landers

Copyright © 2015 by Jenifer Novak Landers

All rights reserved.

No part of this book may be used or reproduced in any manner whatsoever without written permission.

www.greatlittlebook.com

ISBN Paperback # 978-0-9905923-8-9
ISBN Kindle # 978-1-942115-07-6
ISBN ebook # 978-1-942115-08-3

To My Reader

> *"We can choose to stand tall and see life as the colorful and unique mosaic it really is. Perspective is everything."*   -Uta

What if you could watch your life on a movie screen? The movie you are watching is called "You, Fully Expressed Living." Everything you see depends on the perspective you choose to take. The way you choose to see things influences how it plays out. Have you shared a movie or book with a friend who had a completely different experience of it? That's because they came from a different perspective than you did. Perspective is a powerful influence. Know that your perspective is your choice. Always. Imagine that every part of your life-movie is an opportunity to choose a perspective that influences your happiness and fulfillment.

Helping people see things differently is my passion for being a Life Coach. I created this book to help you see yourself in the spotlight of your fullest expression. You, fully expressed! From that perspective, you have room to love yourself more, express yourself more, reach more of your potential, and give more of yourself to the world.

Each article was written to guide you into an experience of fulfillment. Enjoy the journey as you see things differently one article at a time.

Getting stuck in life happens when we see only one perspective. Choosing a higher view, being willing to look from a new angle, or whatever it takes to broaden your original perspective is the way to go from stuck to fulfilled.

Use this book to bring on a positive perspective, make moments matter by taking action, and ultimately move forward with a sense of eager anticipation for fulfillment.

Fully Expressed Living means fulfillment on all levels: Worldly, physically, spiritually, emotionally and mentally.

-Jenifer Novak Landers

Why 50 Ways to See the Bigger Picture?

Choosing to live from inspiring perspectives is a gift to the world. Fifty opportunities to change your perspective is a great start. Let's learn to choose what matters most and then BE our fullest expression of love and presence.

I invite you to take a different approach to your personal development. Rather than working from a list of tasks toward improving your life, this book will help you designate ONE key area to focus on at a time. Make one single shift that comes from your core to accelerate the kind of changes that gives you positive momentum.

This approach helps you create results that are already connected to your soul, making it easier for you to experience fulfillment as you move forward. Think of it like a creative process where one idea sparks another, and another, until the end result is even greater than the progression of sparks.

Follow your gut feelings as you read through each article. Make room for the pieces that stand out to you and use the exercises at the end of each section to find your own personal "Key Focus Area."

I have a talent for listening deeply to my client's stories, always looking for what has heart and meaning. While listening in this deeper way, I illuminate one idea, one possibility, or one perspective and I invite my client to notice where they resonate with it, and ultimately where they can take responsibility for their perspective of choice.

When you can see your circumstances in a detached way, you have made room for a new perspective to appear. You already have the ability to do this for yourself. Just allow it, and keep practicing. Soon you are thriving in the life you want to have.

Intention: Inspire the part of yourself that already KNOWS fulfillment.

Activate the inner wisdom you already have and feed it with empowering perspectives. This book is a collection of fifty articles about life's challenges, opportunities and common milestones we all encounter as human beings. Each article is loaded with ideas and actions you can use to bring whatever your heart desires into the reality of your life.

Imagine each of your life-experiences as a "snapshot" containing everything you need to learn, celebrate or heal. As you collect the "snapshots" along your path, you create the bigger picture of your life. The gift of each snapshot is awareness and perspective. We are here to fully explore ourselves in these precious life experiences. The more we can learn about ourselves, the more room we have to give and receive love.

Fully Expressed Living comes from the heart.

I coach people to dig deeper into their own heart and meaning, to take action from there rather than a cerebral or intellectual level.

The feminine or "right-brain" skills such as empathy, connection and intuition are highly useful for creating fulfillment in our lives. This is our heart. The challenge comes when we typically rely on the traditional masculine or "left brain" skills that access logic, linear thinking and rationality when we are learning something new. This side is in our head. Fully Expressed Living is about what illuminates the balance between each side, where we can logically understand a process or a checklist for achieving fulfillment while at the same time intuitively flowing with the feeling of fulfillment and attracting more of it from there.

We are dancing along in an information-savvy world overflowing with self-improvement information. I see people taking a literal approach to personal growth which causes their conversations to sway away from their natural intuitive and empathic skills. It's similar to the distinction between DOING something and BEING something.

By taking on new perspectives, you can learn the value of raising your consciousness rather than just expanding your mental capacity to hold and assimilate vast quantities of information.

To explore your life, I would ask you first, "Where is your inner wisdom in this?" rather than asking "What do you think about this?"

Freedom occurs when we become present with our inner landscape. Unplug. Be in the moment.

You have a lush garden of possibility inside of yourself, and I am honored to be your guide and coach for this exploration.

I hope this book inspires you to do your personal growth work at your deepest level possible so results will stick and a strong foundation forms for you. Imagine that it's easy

Grab the gumption (which means to take inspired action), and commit to practicing the spiritual perspectives. Most importantly, enjoy your journey!

Are you a human being having a spiritual experience, or are you a spiritual being having a human experience?

Perhaps the answer depends on your perspective. . . .
This is your journey of creating moments that matter.

Contents

Introduction - iii
How to Create Moments that Matter - 1
The Gardening Analogy - 2
Your Fully Expressed Garden - 4
What to Expect from this Book - 5
50 Ways to See the Bigger Picture - 6
Take Action in the Bigger Picture: Do the Exercises - 7
Get Gumption Exercises - 9
Get Unplugged Exercises - 10

SECTION ONE: Expand Your Perspective - 11
What if THIS Year is Your Best Yet? - 12
Do You Fall Apart Easily? - 16
Do You Choose Being Nice Over Being Truthful? - 20
Do You Get Addicted to Your Own Drama? - 24
Do Motivational Quotes Work? - 28
What Do You Need to Feel Satisfied? - 32
Do You Know How to Ask for What You Want? - 35
Are You Self Sabotaging OR Self Loving? - 38
Do you REACT or RESPOND? - 41
Do You Have a Love Affair with Change? - 45

SECTION TWO: See Things Differently - 48
Can Self-Doubt Make You Smarter? - 49
Do You Set Yourself Up to REALLY Reach Your Goals? - 53
Are You a Control Freak? - 57
Are You Emotionally Available? - 61
Can you Change a Naysayer into a Supporter? - 65

Will You LISTEN to Me? - 68
Am I Feeling Intimidated? - 71
Can You "Hold the Space" for Someone? - 75
Uplifting Self-Talk Tips - 78
Do You Wait Until the Last Minute? - 81

SECTION THREE: Broaden Your Horizons - 84
Can My Life Be Easy? - 85
Do You Love Being Asked "A Good Question?" - 88
How Do You Get Past Self Doubt? - 92
Are You Keeping Up With The Jonses? - 95
What Happens When You Are in a Slump? - 99
Am I Creating Distraction or Direction? - 101
Are You Ready for a New Chapter? - 103
Do You Think Too Much? - 106
Are You Easily Offended? - 109
Do You Need to Be Right? - 112

SECTION FOUR: Lift Your Point of View - 115
You Easily Distracted? - 116
How Do We Discover Our Limiting Beliefs? - 119
When is Criticism Your Best Friend? - 122
Do You Make Your Milestones Empowering? - 126
Are You Willing to Simplify Your Desires? - 129
Want More PEACE in Your Life? - 131
Do You Embrace the Power of Trust? - 133
How is Your Self Esteem? - 136
What is Perfect About THIS Moment? - 139
Should I Get Involved? - 142

SECTION FIVE: Visualize the Bigger Picture - 145
Can You "Find the Good" in Any Situation? - 146
Is a Balanced Life REALLY Possible? - 150
What Does it Take to Make Changes Stick? - 154
The Power of an Easy Going Mood - 158
What Makes it Matter? - 161

To Brag or Not to Brag? - 164
Did You Forget You Are a Rock Star? - 167
Why Not Give In? - 170
Do You Have Personal Jet Lag? - 173
Are You Trapped by NOT Wanting Something? - 175

SUMMARY - 178
Own Your Greatest Perspective - 180
Record Your Manifestations - 182
Blocks and Sabotages - 183
FINAL WORDS - 184
About Jenifer Novak Landers - 185
Need a Speaker? - 186
UNPLUGGABLES - 187
Acknowledgements - 188

How to Create Moments that Matter

Each article takes you into life experiences and new ideas for living, all designed to bring out a new perspective.

- Take action on your insights to create change easily and effortlessly.
- Expect to find practical ways to improve your life's journey.
- Embrace the theme of "getting to the heart of things."

Making moments that matter serves you in a transformational way, and your life experience will take on more joy and pleasure as a result.

Life is not supposed to be hard, though we can make it that way with limited thinking, low expectations, or failing to see ourselves as we really are. This is why PERSPECTIVE is a powerful tool. **This is why FULLY EXPRESSED LIVING is a powerful choice.**

We are in charge of how we see things. If the purpose of our life is to express our natural essence which is LOVE, then use this book to rise above what makes your life hard, and connect with what opens your heart to Love.

"The Day you decide you are more interested in being aware of your thoughts than you are in the thoughts themselves – that is the day you will find your way out." -Michal Singer

The Gardening Analogy.

Whether you enjoy gardening, you garden as a hobby or just appreciate a beautiful garden, I love this analogy because it is an easily relatable process.

Start by imagining the enjoyment of sitting your own special garden.
How do you get there?
What do you need?
What would it take?

A "garden" can be many things to many people. Whatever image comes to mind, embrace it as an aspect of your life where you can enjoy the abundance and beauty of fully experiencing yourself and your surroundings.

If you "want to have a garden" in your life, this can represent any goal, desire or dream you have. You need to start somewhere. I use this process with my clients when we are defining what is possible, creating a vision or setting goals to take life to the next level.

The Gardening Analogy helps you find your own deeper meaning every step of the way.

First we must have a vision for the garden. What is the most inspiring and compelling vision you have? Spell it out. Make a picture of it. Collect images that represent every aspect of it.

Next we must prepare the dirt. Dig into the dirt. Turn the soil over. Maybe there will be boulders in the way. Maybe we need to dig up more dirt. We need a nourishing and solid foundation to build upon.

We must have a plan for planting and creating the garden of your dreams. Planting seeds, putting things in place, building it. We will go one step at a time, always noticing what is happening, and what is NOT happening so we can adjust. Are there times we need to re-commit to the vision? Are there times we lose motivation and get stuck in a rut? We will handle these things as part of the process, remembering gratitude and attention on what IS growing and what IS already happening.

Next we embrace the growth and keep moving forward. Soon the garden is in place. Our dream/desire/vision has taken form. We can see the manifestation in front of us.

There will inevitably be weeds that must be pulled. Weeds we didn't notice, or weeds that got out of control. The goal is to detach from anything negative regarding the weeds, and love the cycle and balance of every single component happening as the garden grows. Pulling weeds makes room for the beauty to expand.

Make adjustments and learn what works, while releasing what doesn't work. We begin to notice what calls our attention as our dreams move closer. Now we can see and experience the full manifestation of our garden. Next we acknowledge everything about ourselves and the entire process. Claim this milestone. Be fully present, be fully expressed and be fully grateful.

"If you've never experienced the joy of accomplishing more than you can imagine, plant a garden."   -Robert Brault

Your Fully Expressed Garden

Visualize it. Feel into it. Imagine it in detail.
This is the "garden" of your dreams.

Make a plan. What's needed? What must be done?
Prepare the soil. Dig in. Take Action.
Remove boulders, unwanted rocks.

Overcome obstacles.
Plant seeds. Set intentions.
Create what lines up with your vision.
Maintain Growth. Keep moving forward.
Pull weeds. Surrender to the process.

Embrace the cycles.
Be flexible, be willing to make adjustments.
Hold the perspective that keeps your garden growing.

Enjoy every moment fully.
Practice Gratitude.
Receive the gifts.

Acknowledge yourself every step of the way.

"The glory of gardening: hands in the dirt, head in the sun, heart with nature. To nurture a garden is to feed not just the body but the soul."   —Alfred Austin

How to Be Fully Expressed

Make the most of the exercises that follow each article. Even though this book cannot promise transformation in your life, it IS true that following the suggestions and exercises over the long term will create changes and bring greater fulfillment into your life.

The more you make changes internally, the greater the changes you will see externally.

I watch people shift patterns in their lives simply by making one small change in an approach or a reaction. If they do this consistently over time, changes take root.

May you shine in the spotlight of all your desires.

50 Ways to See the Bigger Picture

I wrote weekly articles for the Folsom Telegraph Newspaper over a period of 2 years. I wanted to offer my readers new ways to think and new ways to see themselves. I wanted to offer new perspectives on personal topics. I included exercises and deeper questions with each article because of my passion for taking action when something matters in our lives.

Let's divide the 50 articles into five sections. After all, your perspective changes as you go along. . . .

ONE: Expand Your Perspective

TWO: See Things Differently

THREE: Broaden Your Horizons

FOUR: Lift Your Point of View

FIVE: Visualize the Bigger Picture

Take Action in the Bigger Picture: Do the Exercises

You will find exercises throughout the book. "Make it matter by taking action" is your new mantra as you read through all five sections.

Fill out every exercise asking for your input. Turn this book into a well-worn companion filled with scribbles and notes to keep as a trusted resource as long as you need it. Use a separate journal for the exercises.

You will find two types of exercises in this book.
The first is the "GET GUMPTION" exercise.
Second is the "GET UNPLUGGED" exercise.

The word GUMPTION is one of my favorites because it describes the type of person I enjoy becoming. Gumption means "taking inspired action." A person with gumption has positive energy, passion for making things happen, is driven toward joyful achievement and is fueled from an inspiring source

GET GUMPTION: Take Inspired Action.

The "Get Gumption" exercise invites you to take inspired action and move forward to create results. Each exercise suggests action steps that are measurable and realistic. Do them.

Use the exercises to activate your own version of GUMPTION and *make some fulfillment happen!*

GET UNPLUGGED: Be Fully Present.

This exercise invites you to access a higher perspective. This is simply your connection to love, or source, or God, or your best self. It's your personal level of connection. The idea is to unplug from anything that distracts you from being fully present.

Unplug from your cell phone or your computer to practice mindfulness and get to know your internal wisdom.

Get Gumption Exercises

> *"Be daring, be different, be impractical. Be anything that will assert integrity of purpose and imaginative vision against the play-it-safers, the creatures of the commonplace, the slaves of the ordinary."*   -Cecil Beaton

Don't be afraid to sit in the front row of your own life.
This is gumption.

Action steps are effective when they are simple, easy and often times unexpected. As you work the "Things to Do" exercises in the book, you may find that your intuition nudges you to do something that doesn't make sense to you at the time. Follow it anyway. Do it anyway. Trust your gut feelings.
This is gumption.

The difference between who you are and who you want to be is based on what you actually DO.

Gumption = Taking Inspired Action.

Choose a notebook or journal to use exclusively as you work through the exercises in this book.

Get Unplugged Exercises

> *Ego says, "Once everything falls into place, I'll feel peace." Spirit says, "Once you find your peace, everything will fall into place."* -Marianne Williamson

The "Get Unplugged" exercises take you into a broader view. Choose to unplug from anything keeping you from being fully present with yourself and the exercise at hand. Taking an "unplugged perspective" makes room for your fulfillment.

"Get Unplugged" means you made the choice to be fully present. Unplugging refers to your cell phone or any technology that pulls attention away from yourself and what is going on around you.

When you "Get Unplugged", magic happens. One of the most transformative questions I ask in my coaching sessions is this: "Where is LOVE in this perspective?"

Use the exercises to get unplugged and make room for the presence of love.

You always have the choice to DO something that feeds your internal flame (the source of energy within you.) Being present and being mindful of the moment ignites this flame.

DO the exercises. Discover practical ways to integrate a spiritual perspective in your life.

SECTION ONE:

Expand Your Perspective

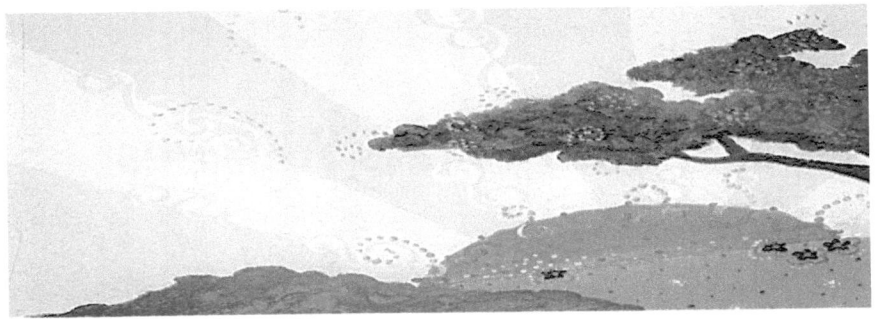

*"The trees, the flowers, the plants grow in silence.
The stars, the sun, the moon move in silence.
Silence gives us a new perspective."*

-Mother Theresa

10 THINGS YOU CAN DO DIFFERENTLY IN THIS SECTION:

- ✔ Have the best year of your life.
- ✔ See falling apart as an event, not a person.
- ✔ Speak from authenticity rather than accommodation.
- ✔ Be free from drama and emotional addictions
- ✔ Motivate yourself from the inside out.
- ✔ Understand the depths of satisfaction and fulfillment.
- ✔ Ask for what you want and get your needs met.
- ✔ Choose self-love over self-sabotage.
- ✔ Respond with grace and resilience when needed.
- ✔ Embrace the joy of change.

1

What if THIS Year is Your Best Yet?

Deciding to live the best year of your life is a mindset. This choice includes contemplating what went well and what fell short. Making a list of successes and failures helps you imagine and plan for changes and improvements throughout the year.

You want to remember what truly matters to you (and to your loved ones and your community and your world.) You want to find ways to hold the "All" in this busy world. When you find yourself stuck or stressed or depressed, it turns out the view from those places is exactly what you need to see in order to step into the best year of your life with renewed gratitude and gumption. Sometimes you wobble and sometimes you soar. The key is not to forget that you are in charge of creating it for yourself.

Let's gather some energy to set yourself on track for the best year of your life. What would you do this month to set yourself up for success next year? This is the perfect time to bring out your "inner child" and be playful with what you would like to do differently, or what you would like to have more of this next year.

Five questions to establish your new "THIS IS THE BEST YEAR OF MY LIFE" mindset:

1. Where am I now?

Check yourself on a scale of 1 – 10. Where is your confidence level regarding changes you'd like to make? Where is your level of well-being? Where is your level of personal awareness? Those three areas are the most influential on your ability to manifest greater things in your life. Where are you in your life or business that is stuck? Can you take a look at what is needed to move yourself from where you are toward the "10" that represents the height of your success and happiness?

2. How did I get here?

Check your prosperity beliefs. Do you have attitudes toward prosperity or financial issues that keep you in a small or limited place? Check your leadership beliefs. Do you have a perspective on yourself or others that empowers you to be all you can be? Are you easily able to access your personal leadership in your relationships, your work, and your social activities? What is the mindset that created your scene this year? Get clear with these aspects, and your success mindset follows.

3. Where would I like to be?

Do you feel on purpose with yourself and with your work? Have you or will you take the time to designate a specific vision for your life or business? If this vision is compelling and inspiring to you, then you are much farther along the path toward your best year yet. Are you setting goals for 2014 that are specific for your lifestyle, contribution, health, family, fun, finances, and relationships? Asking this question to the many areas of our lives can be a fun activity to share with someone close to you. Make a date with some big sheets of paper, some markers and hold each other accountable as you go along.

4. What should I do more of? And what should I do less of?

Make a list of what worked for you this year. Next make a list of what did not work for you this year. The top 3-4 things on each of those lists indicate what you can shift. Did you follow your intuition this year? Did you take the risks you needed to take this year? These are the top areas where you can increase or decrease spending your precious energy. Make all your choices matter, and your year will automatically grow in success.

5. What ways can I get from where I am to where I want to be?

Here is the secret sauce factor: Have an accountability structure. This looks like a system or a calendar or an environment that keeps you productive and on track. It also can look like another person or a mentor or a coach who understands your goals and commitments and holds you accountable to them. When you have measurable ways to go from stepping stone to stepping stone, the experience of moving forward along the path stays clear and keeps your tank fueled.

You deserve your best year EVER. Imagine who is touched when you are the best you can be.

It's a beautiful path through your inner landscape. Even if you make one small change based on these suggestions, you can watch your life become more and more colorful along the way.

EXERCISES

GET GUMPTION: Take Inspired Action.

Share your goals and dreams with another significant person in your life.

JOURNAL THIS:

- ◊ If money and time were no object, what would your self-care care routine look like?
  Describe this in detail.
- ◊ Who benefits from your self-care priority and why?
  List a minimum of three significant people in your life

GET UNPLUGGED: Be Fully Present

Imagine you are at the end of your best year yet. Imagine you are being interviewed by someone famous, even on television. You are sharing about your year. Your body feels grounded and relaxed. Your energy is vibrant. Feel deeply into this state.

MEDITATE THIS:

- ◊ I am celebrating myself and want to GIVE!
- ◊ I have everything I need for my best year yet.

2

Do You Fall Apart Easily?

We all fall apart. Without judging it as a "bad" thing, we can celebrate the chance to put ourselves back together in an even grander version, or certainly in a way that is better or more joyful than what was going on when the falling apart occurred. . . so let's get excited and say, "BRING IT!"

How can you avoid getting sidelined when you fall apart?

When children play, the "falling apart" is often the most fun part of the game! I remember my daughter squealing with delight when we would "all fall down" and then get back up and start twirling around again. It was FUN when the tower of blocks fell down, and it was FUN to laugh when a cartoon character fell apart and then bounced back.

Recall a specific example where you recently fell apart. Did you pretend you still had it together? What didn't go your way? When plans abruptly change and you are left holding the ball, how well do you manage your own energy? Have you ever fallen apart when your expectations are not met? Yes yes, and yes.

I watched a friend fall apart this week when her flight got cancelled. The ability to adjust quickly when circumstances are not in your control is an artful way to live. I admired her choice to process the emotions and quickly land on a new perspective for the situation that she could feel excited and positive about. Easy? Not always. But we always get to improve our ability to "turn on a dime". Resiliency. Self-Reliance.

Another client fell apart when his son wasn't going to arrive in time. A friend continuously falls apart because she is adjusting to her divorced and co-parenting lifestyle. . .

What if we just planned on falling apart every day?

Now look at the experience you have when you watch someone else fall apart. Are you patient with them? Frustrated? Detached? Notice if you wish they would "get it together" or make adjustments quicker or more effectively. Whatever you wish for them, is the exact message you would whisper in your own ear. *Be your own angel and give that wisdom or support back to yourself.*

> *"The key to resilience is a healthy and strong level of self-awareness."*   -Brene' Brown

Brene' Brown has become a popular speaker and author with her research-based perspective about embracing our imperfections in order to live a whole-hearted life, a fulfilled life. Her work shows us the requirement for a higher levels of self-awareness as we all work to improve our lives. The MORE we can know and understand about ourselves, the more we have to rely on when life throws us a curve ball.

Since you are the only one growing your self-awareness, YOU are the one in charge of building it. You can make deposits in to your self-awareness bank account until you are wealthy beyond measure.

How? By reading books, studying personal development materials, listening to talks or watching videos by thought leaders, attending workshops or seminars, participating in church or consciousness-raising activities.

The more self-aware you are, the easier it is to bounce back. It's easier to re-frame a challenge into an opportunity. It's easier to see the silver lining FIRST. It's easier to choose what feels good over the drama or negativity. If your path is about expanding your awareness, then you have so much more room to play.

Imagine your self-awareness as a treasure chest in a childhood bedroom: If it's filled to the brim with tools, possibilities and treasures, and you've got endless possibilities. Keep changing and adding to the contents. Keep it current with your life.

EXERCISES

GET GUMPTION: Take Inspired Action.

Get a box or container to use as a treasure chest. Find one or two special items to put inside. (Example: A stone that reminds you of strength, a bead or piece of jewelry that reminds you of self-awareness, or a tiny figurine or statue that reminds you of your inner warrior.)

JOURNAL THIS:

- ◊ What happens when you "fall apart"?
- ◊ How can you make it easier to bounce back?

GET UNPLUGGED: Be Fully Present

Let yourself settle, and remember that deep inside you are simply a witness. You are silent and aware. When you become quiet inside, it's like a channel is opening from the outside edges into the center of your viewpoint. This helps you become detached, and a new awareness begins to enter. Notice this new perspective.

MEDITATE THIS:

- ◊ As I release any tension in my body, my mind relaxes.
- ◊ My awareness is growing because I am allowing it.

3

Do You Choose Being Nice Over Being Truthful?

It's time for a NICE-Over. This old business of "being nice" has lost its luster. Lost its value. It's becoming quite useless in today's scene.

A client sat in my office last week wrestling with her choice to either "Be NICE to keep the peace, OR, to take a stand and bring it to an end." How often do we face the very same choice point? We need to end a relationship that's no longer working, we need to fire a client, we need to ask an employee to change, we need to invite someone in or invite them out, or we just simply need to make a change happen.

Considering that we are surrounded by influences that force us to raise our consciousness every day, this business of "Making Nice" is up for change. Question your values at the core. Is NICE the way to demonstrate your authenticity? Is NICE the way to send the message from your integrity? Who are you really being, when you are taking the role of "being nice"??

If your choice to "Be Nice" is lined up with the values you are committed to expressing, then you are on track. If you notice that you are compromising or abandoning your values, then HOORAY, you just stepped into a huge growth moment.

In the light of raising our consciousness, notice how "Making

Nice" is actually small, or flat, or certainly limited in many ways. Consciousness includes asking, "How can I serve?" So look at each moment you make a choice and ask, "Does this action or thought *make nice* or does it inspire greater service (to myself and others?)." Are you feeling expanded already?

I helped my client get quiet with a meditation and then see with clarity that facing the risk of ending a business relationship served in a bigger way than taking the role of Peace-Maker and hoping to keep everyone feeling "Nice". . . We talked about which messages she is sending (to herself and to everyone involved) by choosing to keep the peace, and which message is sent by taking a stand. Great perspective!

Check your personal beliefs. Is it hard to be confrontational? Is it easier to be nice? Do you believe that taking a stand will bring you a loss of some kind? And is that loss wrong or bad somehow? Maybe you are telling yourself a certain story about how it will be. Just see if you can tell a different story.

We all take the side of nice in different areas of our lives. Over there, it's easy to take a stand. Over here, it's brutally difficult! Sometimes we are naturally in a leadership role, and sometimes we are in a natural following role. Being NICE typically lives in a following role. If you notice a place in your life where you need to take more leadership, start by letting go of your need to keep the peace, or your "Nice" comfort zone.

The countless times I have taken the opportunity to be bold with my feedback, or call someone out, or say it boldly as I see it, it's a victory for growth every time. It's a celebration of truth and moving forward. At first, it felt wobbly and scary, but quickly that fades into confidence and even excited anticipation for the next opportunity!

The joy of being in service to another person or another situation by stepping outside of "Being Nice" feels fullfilling. My clients depend on me to deliver the hard core feedback. If I wasn't being authentic by reflecting what I see honestly, we would all miss huge chances to grow or celebrate.

It's time for you to embrace the expanded part of you that wants a larger role.

Beyond the quality of *nice*, you can find powerful qualities such as: Bold, Brave, Edgy, Influential, Effective, Genuine, Compassionate and Awesome. We are well versed in all of these qualities, but often we default into a few that have become our comfort zone.

Today's relationships and personal situations require our expanded selves to come forward. Bye-Bye Nice. Hello new role, and hello better results. Hello lasting change for the better.

Two powerful questions to shift the relationship you have with "Being Nice":

ONE: *"If keeping the peace was NOT my role, what would I be doing instead?"* **TWO:** *"If I had no fear in this situation, what would I do?"*

Dig into these questions. There will be treasure for sure.

EXERCISES

GET GUMPTION: Take Inspired Action

Ask someone you trust for feedback on where you play small or where you do "nice"?

JOURNAL THIS:

What are two new qualities you can express this week?

If you committed to this statement, "I Choose to Take a Stand", where would you do it? With who?

GET UNPLUGGED: Be Fully Present

Give yourself time to Unplug every day. This is your new ritual to take a stand for yourself and honor your inner wisdom. Choose to unplug for awhile, and let the magic happen.

MEDITATE THIS:

Meditate while holding a beautiful flower. See that the flower is "taking a stand" with authenticity and grace.

See that the flower doesn't play small.

See yourself as a fully expressed flower.

4

Do You Get Addicted to Your Own Drama?

The dinner table was a lively place in my family growing up. Conversation flowed with laughter and connection and we all enjoyed expressing ourselves together. My Dad was a passionate story-teller and was always ready with witty come-backs. He often would shout out, "COLOR!" to indicate that someone was exaggerating their story. Then it became humorous to shout it out even when the story was factual. Sometimes the more "COLOR" in a story, the better. And sometimes, it stopped you in your tracks if you were just creating drama.

Where do you add "COLOR!" to your expressions or experiences? It's fine to add some spice or dazzle to a story. Creative writing is a perfect example of valuable exaggeration. The trouble starts when you exaggerate and create stress, pain and unrest as a result.

Do you have a tendency to exaggerate every little thing that happens to you? If you add "COLOR" to the bad things, you are especially prone to a drama addiction.

Notice the unnecessary stress you are adding to your life (and the people around you) with your exaggerations. Do you sometimes make it feel like "the end of the world" when you face a difficulty?

Three RED FLAGS for Drama Addiction:

Red flag number one for drama addiction: Using the "I'm Just Joking" excuse. Are your comments based on an exaggerated view of someone or something? Where are you coming from when you have to mitigate with a "just joking" clause? Drama.

Watch your own ways of thinking and talking. If you think you are just being playful or sarcastic for fun, balance your choice with the understanding that when we say things repeatedly our mind takes it as real.

Red flag number two for drama addiction: Do you inflate the frequency of something happening to you? I have a client who says, "I always fall behind because I get distracted!" or "Dating is always awkward!" Obviously she is only remembering the bad times, and forgetting all the times it wasn't bad (or went well). Is it ever true that something *always* happens to you? Highly unlikely. Unless you are addicted to the drama . . . and then, yes, it's true.

A friend of mine created a saying to use in our relationship where we could call out this kind of dramatized thinking. We would interrupt each other by saying, "Distortion!" and then look for at least one past example or situation that proves it wrong.

Often times we would call each other and start the conversation by saying, "I'm having a distortion!" and then support each other to get a better perspective. Pretty soon it became obvious when one of us was choosing to promote the drama of the situation rather than the reality of it. Try this with someone who has earned your trust.

Red flag number three that you are addicted to your own drama: Do you make something WAY more important than it really is? Think of situations in your life that you are able to look back on and say, "I thought it was such a big deal at the time, but it wasn't really at all!" Addicted to your own drama means that you are likely to make things out to be worse than they really are, and your experience of the situation is now much more painful and stressful.

A good drama addict will tell the same story two or three more times and then the minimal stress that could have been released in the moment is now something bigger and stronger than ever.

Avoid creating drama by learning to let go of the small stuff and not creating a tragedy out of every story. These type of exaggerations can become unhealthy and definitely do not contribute to a life moving forward.

Our personal drama is mostly connected to over-reactive thinking. The good news is that we can practice letting go of these types of thoughts. Stop jumping to conclusions rather than suspending your judgment until you have proper facts and understanding.

Notice your tendency to make these types of statements: "I'm 100% sure" or "I know as a matter of fact" or "There's no way that happened." Ask yourself if you can really know that it's true.

Usually the truth is that you do not know for sure what is true. Your drama addiction kicks in when you choose to activate any of those "I know for sure" statements. Jumping to conclusions leads to a lot of unnecessary stress.

EXERCISES

GET GUMPTION

Play the "Or Not" game with yourself.

Take one full day and say the words, "Or Not" after EVERYTHING you hear or say. (Keeping it to yourself is fine.) Notice what's different.

JOURNAL THIS:

- List ten things you THINK are true.
- Now list one reason for each why you do not know for sure that it's true. What perspective do you have when you can prove yourself wrong?

GET UNPLUGGED

Make room for surrender, peace and honoring the ordinary pleasures of each day/moment. Allowing things to unravel can be the greatest gift of peace into our lives. Be playful with this.

MEDITATE THIS:

- No matter how I feel or what happens, I can choose to awaken every morning in gratitude and joy.
- I am willing to take responsibility for my own simplicity; heart, mind and soul.

5

Do Motivational Quotes Work?

Where do you get a fix of inspiration?

How do you evolve your own philosophy of life?

A breakthrough or revelation can come from our own lives, or it can come from another perspective such as films, books, art or... motivational quotes.

We want to be motivated and we need to see positive results in order to stay motivated, so how can we be consistent rather than a fleeting moment from the quote-of-the-day?

We have access to a treasure chest of inspirational resources in life that help us stay motivated along our way. Do you notice that Facebook and Pinterest are full of motivational quotes fully decorated with backgrounds and photos? Participants in these two social media sites take turns dazzling each other with motivational postings about how to be more, do better, stay happy, and enjoy life. The Pinterest website is hugely popular for collections of motivational images, quotes, posters, and artfully illustrated inspirational words. It's fun, it's a pleasure-addiction, and yet, none of these things really work. Only you work.

It is your REACTION to motivational quotes that makes them work.

Read a motivational quote and use your awareness to ask, "What do I make this mean?"

Your answer indicates what truly motivates you.

Ask yourself three questions to take it a step further:

What does it mean about me?
What does it mean about my relationships?
What does it mean for my success?

Your answers reveal your ability to motivate yourself no matter what is going on.

Motivation and inspiration have longer lasting results when they are sourced within us. A motivational quote or image is external. We see it outside of ourselves. Now is the time to take it internally. Go within.

> *"What you get by reaching your destination is not nearly as important as what you will become."*   -Zig Ziglar

Listen to the story you tell yourself ABOUT the quote. Listen for where the quote connects you to positive energy.

Now you can see why it's not about the motivational quote. It's about what you DO with it. How you process it both intellectually and emotionally.

Author Mitch Albom offers this motivational quote: *"All endings are also beginnings."* Start looking at how this applies to a personal situation in your life today. Look for how it's relevant to your challenges or triumphs? Notice if it inspires you and why.

A motivational quote doesn't work if you resist it, oppose it, or are unwilling to apply it. These quotes can sometimes elicit more self-doubt than self-satisfaction.

EXERCISES

GET GUMPTION

Go to Pinterest or Google Images and print out 3 motivational quotes that catch your eye. Place each quote on a separate page and rewrite it in your own words, or add something personal to it. Then sign YOUR name after the quote.

JOURNAL THIS:

Practice re-framing your thoughts as you respond to the following motivational quotes.

- ◊ List three to five pieces of advice you typically give to other people.
- ◊ What do you tell others to encourage them?
- ◊ Now NOTICE where these things apply to you.
  Re-write all of them as personal messages to yourself. Sign each one.

GET UNPLUGGED

If you have found your truth within yourself there is nothing more in life to find. Truth is fully expressed through you.

MEDITATE THIS:

Look at a candle for five minutes:

- ◊ My truth looks like a ray of light coming from beyond into any dark places in my world. Look at a candle.
- ◊ I love knowing that my inner flame is there to motivate me anytime I remember to connect with it.

6

What Do You Need to Feel Satisfied?

What are we really looking for in life? Top answers include happiness, fulfillment, meaning, purpose, and did I mention happiness? All of these things, and others we could add to the list contribute to the ease of our lives.

If you had more happiness and fulfillment in your life, would you say life was easier? If your life had more meaning and joy, would you say that life feels easy? Do you equate easy with satisfying?

Think of the qualities you associate with "life being easy". Maybe your needs would be met. Maybe the areas of your life that are challenging would become more peaceful and harmonious. Maybe your relationships would have greater focus on appreciation and gratitude rather than struggle and resistance.

I worked with a client last week on the understanding of polarity. When issues and feelings swing between extreme opposites, there is room between them where we can choose our standing place, and there is room to experience fullness rather than limitation. A standard definition of polarity is, "the condition of opposing extremes." Examples of polarity in life could include happy and sad, light and dark, love and fear. One client was super stuck in his imbalance of work and family life. How can he find time and energy to be successful in both? When we looked at the polarity of enjoying a life that was messy AND focused, he was able to make more room and then he found connection with feeling that "life is easier."

I love the power of using simple tools. Looking for ways to make life easier could be the simplest way for you to transform areas where your joy has been sucked away or your fulfillment has been overcome by challenges. A powerful question to ask yourself on a daily basis is, "What would make this EASIER?" Use the question when you are in the stress of your day. Use it when you are anticipating something you need to show up for or handle.

Let's take a minute to laugh at ourselves for how silly it is to NOT take the time to make everything we do easier (more enjoyable, more meaningful). Notice if you think that taking an easier approach is negative somehow. If you make it mean that easy is lazy, you will resist this tool for change. If you make it mean that taking something easy is not honorable, or not good enough, then you have completely sabotaged your potential for a positive new experience.

Make your life easier. Make it mean that easy is spiritual. Or easy is freedom. Or that easy is about tenderness, acceptance and an open heart. Better yet, make a list of the qualities you most want to be known for in your life, and then associate ALL of them with the idea that you are choosing to "make your life easier". The only real meaning is in the story you choose to tell yourself.

Six practical tips to make your life easier:

1. Make the present moment your new best friend. Spend all your time with it.

2. Eliminate Blame. Better yet, annihilate it. Change things by DOING instead of blaming or excusing someone else.

3. Shout from your inner mountain top: "Who Cares What They

Think?" Focus on your inner inspiration instead of other people's opinions.

4. Get a negativity buster. Just stop being negative! (Thinking negative, expecting negative, seeing negative)

5. Be easy on YOURSELF. Fire yourself from criticizing. Stop informing yourself of shortcomings and inadequacies.

6. Fall in love with fearless. Do something that makes you a little uncomfortable every day to develop your confidence.

Choose things that are simple and easily achievable.

It's much better to improve your life by taking super small steps that slowly make a difference. You can build on positive change when you have the time and space to see it and embrace how it happens for you.

Make your life easier by letting go of everything in the way of just allowing yourself to experience the each moment.

Maybe it's easier to slow down. Maybe it's easier to push forward. Your own inner wisdom is the only thing you need to hear and honor.

YOU are the one who makes it easier.

7

Do You Know How to Ask for What You Want?

Do you know people who get exactly what they want every time they ask?

It's important to ask directly for what you want, and you must be specific about what you hope to achieve.

A successful life includes knowing how to ask. Take on this skill and you will see great results. Make asking easier by creating a script for what you want. Along with the script, you must decide to do it no matter what. The more clarity you have, the better your chances at getting your needs met. When you are clear, it's actually easier to ask!

Amanda Palmer, author of *The Art of Asking* says that asking makes us vulnerable. "To ask for something is human; to want something and ask someone else for it requires a connection."

When we feel a connection we naturally want to help. Do not avoid being open and vulnerable. The world needs more of this.

Don't make people figure it out. So many people will talk in circles, or send emails "just to say hello" or fumble around their idea instead of being clear about what they want. Do you ever notice that you are secretly hoping the other person will see your desire and reach out to help you?

Simple truth: Getting what you want requires asking for it, and you must be clear, direct and specific about what you want.

Here is a formula to make an "easy ask": Define your problem. Outline what you want. Determine who you can connect with, and give them enough information to understand what is being asked of them.

Decide how many times you will ask. Once? Twice? More?

Are you repeating yourself?

What if you were not afraid to ask someone more than once?

What if every time you ask, you have better chances of getting what you want?

You. Simply. Must. Ask.

Practice makes perfect. Every time you ask you are practicing for a bigger ask. What can you learn from each time you ask?

Communicate your gratitude or the results you got from asking. Now you've given your ask greater value. You have allowed someone else the opportunity to be of service. We all love to be kind and helpful.

Timing is everything. People get worn out. Don't ask when someone is already at the end of their reserves. Be smart about when you ask. Another important skill is to stay silent afterward.

Ask from you heart, and then return to your heart and simply wait. Too many people trash the space after they ask with filler words, when silence is what is needed. You must give the other person space to consider your desires and respond thoughtfully. If we speak again too quickly we risk the chance of pushing them toward NO.

Use positive body language when you ask. This is naturally easy to do if you are coming from your heart. Be relaxed, look relaxed and be fully present.

Think positive. What if you assumed that the other person actually wants to help you? What if you assumed that they are delighted and are just waiting for you to ask?

The only thing in the way of getting what you want, is your own choice to ask. Add in your fear of hearing the dreaded word, "NO" and you are stuck.

Consider this perspective: By not asking, you have already chosen "no" as the outcome. Each time you hold yourself back from asking for what you want, you give yourself the answer you fear most. Chances are, when you stand up and ask, you will experience a positive result.

8

Are You Self Sabotaging OR Self Loving?

Debbie Ford, best selling author was one of my favorite teachers and mentors along my path. I recommend her book, "The Right Questions" for a further look into this topic and other powerful questions we can ask ourselves to empower our lives. Her books have expanded my perspective and I am grateful for getting to learn from her and participate in her workshops. This article is inspired by her book and I dedicate it to my fond memories and appreciation of her work.

Every choice, action or thought we have is either self-loving or self-sabotaging. There is no in between. Be willing to ask yourself the question, "Am I doing something self-loving, or am I doing something self-sabotaging?" By uncovering your core motivation, you can stay true to what you really say you want.

We are brilliant when it comes to sabotaging ourselves. At every turn, every opportunity and when we least expect it, we can subconsciously choose against what we say we really want. If you ever wonder about your ability to be extremely creative, just notice the part of you that sabotages yourself and you will find a fiercely committed and highly creative force that gets what it wants no matter what!

The key to setting yourself free from sabotaging behaviors that rob you of the life you want to have is to expose the core motivation that drives you in every situation. I work with my clients to break the pattern of stress and struggle about saying they want one thing and doing another, and feeling powerless for not being able to attain the future they desire.

Four ways we sabotage what we say we want.

EXAMPLE ONE:

She wants to lower sugar intake and put only healthy foods into her body. She finds herself at Starbucks (or any indulgence of choice) and notices she's about to make a choice that will either empower her or disempower her. She's about to have a drink filled with sugar and calories. Her intellect says, "It's only one. . . " And her emotions say, "but it makes me feel comforted and cared for!" This type of internal struggle happens everywhere in our lives. When she started asking herself, "Am I being self-loving or self-sabotaging?" she could see the high calorie drink as a wrong choice. Her core motivation was to receive the feeling of comfort she gets from the drink. Because her desire for comfort and feeling cared is driving her, she will fill those needs first before anything else she says she wants. Instead, she can make the choice to slow down and give herself the feeling of care and comfort in a direct way (rather than through the indulgence.) If she blindly follows her core motivation for comfort, she will override her desire for healthy eating and go for the quick fix. Then she moves farther away from her true desires, and even gets to beat herself up afterward!

EXAMPLE TWO:

He wants to have deeper intimacy and a fulfilling sexual relationship. Every time the opportunity arises, he finds a reason to avoid being intimate. If he looked deeper, he would see a core motivation to punish for not giving him what he wants in other areas. What better way to "prove his point" than to take himself away instead of creating closeness? His core motivation wins out. If core motivations are not made conscious, they will override any other desires.

EXAMPLE THREE:

She wants to have discipline and structure in her life, but she is always in a state of chaos because her core motivation is to be a free spirit.

EXAMPLE FOUR:

He decided that he cannot trust anyone and that it's easier to be alone. Even though he says he wants a great relationship in his life, he always chooses the wrong mate because his core motivation is to be by himself.

When you get clear on your core motivation, you can see how every choice you have been making is truly lined up with it. You have been creating EXACTLY what you are most motivated about. When your perspective opens up, you will experience a profound shift in the way you feel about yourself.

It's fun to use perspective to turn your life around!

EXERCISES

Four steps to reveal your core motivations:

> **ONE:** Write down a goal you haven't been able to achieve.
> **TWO:** Make a list of the actions you take AND the actions you do not take that defeat this goal.
> **THREE:** Make a list of the choices you make that take you away from your goal.
> **FOUR:** Look at the list and discover what those actions and choices represent.

When you discipline yourself to ask this powerful question in your daily life, "Am I sabotaging myself or am I loving myself?" you will have an easier time getting the results you say you want in your life.

9

Do you REACT or RESPOND?

The art of maintaining your center in a tough conversation is well worth pursuing. Do you occasionally feel "thrown off guard" interacting with others? One of my clients made a big transition from selling her small business to taking a high profile job with a large corporation in her industry. I asked her what skill or mindset would most benefit her as she started her first week on the job. She quickly answered, "I would like to handle incoming communications with ease and grace, rather than getting ruffled or defensive."

We talked about the waste of energy that occurs when she has a REACTION to someone, rather than being able to RESPOND with grace. The goal is to use energy to stay grounded and focused on positive outcomes.

Our reactions are emotionally based, and more prone to escalate out of control, while our responses are balanced mentally and emotionally from a place of confidence and calm.

We agreed on a personal mantra she could use to support her to express ease and grace. She chose, "I love communicating from my graceful self."

Fully Expressed Living

Five powerful steps you can take to RESPOND gracefully.

1. Recall an experience where you were verbally challenged and did not handle the situation the way you would have liked.
2. Make a list of the qualities you noticed in yourself when the conversation challenged you.
3. Notice if there was a specific trigger that set off your messy REACTION.
4. Make a new list of the qualities you would RATHER express in similar conversations.
(Hint: List qualities that are the direct opposites to your list of step #2.)

5. Look for ways to cultivate those qualities so you are ready to practice them on the spot next time you are verbally challenged.

Practice makes perfect!

Change your perspective on conversations that are challenging.

One option is to see them as a game of "verbal volleyball" where you are responding with your best shot each time. Would you feel more peaceful and confident if you were able to master verbal challenges? Would you have more energy? Give yourself the challenge of taking this on. Imagine someone you know who is masterful in this area. What is one quality you would use to describe that person? Write that quality on your screen saver, or your phone reminder, or on post it notes around your desk area and fully express it this week. This will fuel your ability to conquer any verbal challenge.

Conflict in life is inevitable. We love conflict because it helps us grow! Why not have some FUN with verbal challenges. Keep in mind, these challenges can be delivered in person, or in written communications, or even over voicemail.

Focus on making them fun by applying the following examples to your personal or professional life:

Here is an exchange between Churchill and Lady Astor. This is a great example because it's from a time when wit and cleverness were a valued part of conversation.

She said, "If you were my husband I'd give you poison," and he said, "If you were my wife I'd drink it." What if Lady Astor got ruffled or sidetracked into her own drama with this challenge by Churchill? She stayed present, she held her truth. She played "verbal volleyball" and they both win.

Notice how George Bernard Shaw delivers a verbal challenge to Churchill in this exchange:

"I am enclosing two tickets to the first night of my new play; bring a friend…. if you have one." Churchill's response, "I cannot possibly attend first night, but I will attend the second… if there is one."

When we REACT instead of RESPOND, we are indulging in defensiveness, or judgment or being self-absorbed. Look for internal reactions such as, "how dare you say that!" or "you have no right to talk to me that way!" because such reactions indicate that you will say or do something you will regret. This will deplete your energy and rob you of good feelings and self-confidence.

When we remember who we are, and choose to RESPOND to a challenge with open heart, being neutral and conjuring up our best wit and humor, we create positive results for all involved. RESPONDING is about being of service, and holding all involved in their greatest selves. Communication is a lot like verbal volleyball. Practice your skills. Improve your game.

Here is another example to inspire your new conversational skills: A heated confrontation takes place in the House of Parliament. One member responds to Benjamin Disraeli, leader of the House of Commons. "Sir, you will either die on the gallows or you will die of some unspeakable disease. Disraeli says, "That depends, Sir, on whether I embrace your policies or your mistress."

EXERCISES

What do you notice about yourself when you consider these humorous examples?

Do you see yourself enjoying this new positioning?

Where can you add humor to your communications?

10

Do You Have a Love Affair with Change?

How do you get ready for changes? Do you work to keep things steady? Do you fear certain consequences that come with making a change? Dealing with change is a huge factor in the success of our lives. Notice how you resist or embrace change, your ability to create change or how you help others through change. Changes are part of every stage in our lives beginning in childhood and throughout adult choices, during relationships, parenting, career paths, contributions, and more.

A quote that has stayed with me since college is, *"Change is the Only Constant."* It speaks to my fascination with growth and potential and I loved the way it invites me to let go of my resistance or fears around change.

How can you embrace the ever-changing nature of life with more joy and more peace?

Five stages you can work through to make any change effective:

DENIAL. Do you get defensive when people mention something you do too much or don't do enough? Those are great clues for noticing your denial, and using it to see the need for change. Are you stubbornly resisting a needed change? The truth about denial is that the pain we hold around "avoiding change" is greater than the pain we anticipate around making the change. Facing reality holds the rewards, not the emptiness of denial.

CONTEMPLATION. When denial is overtaken by the lightbulb of clarity, it's a good thing to start patiently playing around with the idea of change. Take the time to weigh out your options and possible choices against the things that are keeping you stuck. This stage is a great time to communicate your ideas or intentions about change with others who have earned your trust. Now you are ready for the next stage.

PREPARATION. It's time to explore all of your options. This stage goes quickly if you simply explore all of your choices and possibilities and make a checklist of everything you need around the change. Look for everything that supports you and gives you the tools or structure needed to have a successful experience with change. This stage is about your plan of action. Make decisions about what you need and who can support you.

ACTION. Five stars for this stage. You can appreciate all the benefits of working through the first three stages by noticing the increase in your strength, your willingness and your resolve to embrace change in a positive way. Now, it's time to "Go for it." Make change happen.

ACKNOWLEDGEMENT. By acknowledging ourselves for positive steps we have taken, the changes become solidified. Get used to claiming your changes. This is hard or unusual for most of us, because we are not used to honoring ourselves in this way. Acknowledge yourself for successes, big or small and build on the momentum. If you fall back into the rut of resistance, or an old pattern, simply acknowledge that it's a normal part of your process. Acknowledge that this relapse is a way to fully integrate your changes into your life for the long term. Mastering the art of self-acknowledgement goes a long way toward resiliency and greater happiness in our changing lives.

I encourage you to embrace change with a passion. There are huge gifts on the other side of your fear or resistance. My favorite gift of change is knowing that I am unique and that no one but me is better equipped to create the life I want.

Another gift of embracing change is to know that you are infinitely resourceful. By going through the stages of change, you prove to yourself that you are capable of more than you usually achieve. I love it when my clients allow themselves to take control of their lives and get even better results.

SECTION TWO:
See Things Differently

"One's destination is never a place, but a new way of seeing things."

–Henry Miller

THIS SECTION INCLUDES POINTS OF VIEW TO HELP YOU:

- ✓ Transform self-doubt into courage.
- ✓ Reach your goals with ease and confidence.
- ✓ Overcome your need to be in control.
- ✓ Express emotional availability.
- ✓ Turn criticism into support.
- ✓ Be a masterful listener.
- ✓ Stand in your power even if you doubt yourself.
- ✓ Support and hold someone as fully capable.
- ✓ Talk to yourself in loving and uplifting ways.
- ✓ See procrastination as a gift or helpful method.

11

Can Self-Doubt Make You Smarter?

Do you doubt yourself? Let's explore new possibilities for embracing our tendency to doubt, and how to use it for victory.

From a personal development perspective, when you do the work to transform your doubt into a positive effort, you are flexing muscles of courage and resilience. You are committing yourself to seeing the bigger picture and taking the higher road. Those "muscles" are extremely valuable to your success in life. Overcoming doubt is now your path of power.

To quote a Proverb: *"Doubt is the beginning not the end of wisdom."*

Make the most of this article by bringing to mind an area where you doubt yourself so that you can personalize the information. Do you hesitate to believe in your talents? Do you feel uncertain about your ability to ask for what you want? Or do you doubt yourself in your relationships or your work? Do you doubt you will ever reach your dream?

Every person experiences doubt at some point. It's defined as "a feeling of uncertainty about the truth, reality or the nature of something. Often we are expected to "show up" assured and firm whether at church, at work or with extended family. Have you experienced being chastised if you admit your weakness and failure? No wonder we choose certainty and cheerfulness rather than expose our secret hurt or doubt. I invite you to use doubt as an opportunity to be authentic and open. (People LOVE us when we are transparent!)

Notice where in your life you are least likely to show up in uncertainty. Coach yourself toward overcoming doubt, and allow doubt to bring out your willingness to question with curiosity.

Doubt feels like a nagging voice that tells you all the reasons you can't succeed. You can call it shyness, anxiety, or lack of self-confidence, but whatever its name, it can hurt your life.

How can we use it in our favor?

First, open your mind with these three quotations:

> *"The quest for certainty blocks the search for meaning. Uncertainty is the very condition to impel man to unfold his powers." - Erich Fromm*
> *"Uncertainty will always be part of the taking charge process." - Harold S. Geneen*
> *"I am certain there is too much certainty in the world." - Michael Crichton*

Now you can shift your perspective to see why doubting is a smart thing to do.

Three positive qualities that indicate doubt is smart:

1. Obedience

The story of Mother Teresa shows us that despite experiencing many days of dark doubt, she continued to serve the people around her. Does it inspire you to see obedience in the face of doubt as the strongest indicator of character and courage?

2. Humility

Smart doubting starts with humility - from our acknowledgment that we haven't got everything figured out, we are willing to admit we can be wrong, and we make it a priority to think critically about our beliefs. If we do not question our beliefs, we are arrogant and prideful, unwilling to change our minds even when it's the right thing to do.

3. Love

Love should be our motivation behind everything, particularly doubt. When we are connected to LOVE, it's easier to work through uncertainty rather than resisting it. When we "Love Thy Neighbor" we can look at ourselves with compassion in order to care for others above all else.

Author of "A History of Doubt", Jennifer Michael Hecht celebrates doubt as an engine of creativity. She reminds us that "Confucius, Socrates, St. Augustine, Galileo and Frederick Douglass were just a few of the innovators who left their mark on history by challenging conventional wisdom."

Give your doubting self a break from the judgments that erode your self-esteem and instead remind yourself that doubt leads to curiosity, exploration and greater successes.

E X E R C I S E S

GET GUMPTION

Play the "I doubt it" game with yourself.

Take one full day and say the words, "I doubt it" after EVERYTHING you hear or say. (Keeping it to yourself is fine.) Notice your new perspective.

JOURNAL THIS:

- ◊ What are ten things you would NEVER want to change in your life?
- ◊ Now list ten ways you would be open to changing them *if you knew it would get you what you want*.

GET UNPLUGGED

Say this to yourself: *"As I am willing to accept more of myself, I am willing to accept more of you."* Make room to embrace the bigger picture of who you are.

MEDITATE THIS:

- ◊ Imagine you are resting in the center of a huge flower that is fully opened to the warmth of the sun. What part of yourself needs to open into self-acceptance?

12

Do You Set Yourself Up to REALLY Reach Your Goals?

Setting goals is great, but setting yourself up to actually achieve them is more important. When you set goals, you demonstrate that you are not just letting life happen to you. Studies show that working toward goals makes people happier.

One of our greatest needs is for a sense of meaning and purpose in life, and setting goals is the first step toward fulfillment.

Staying on track with your goals doesn't come naturally to most of us. Perhaps it's just part of the human design. We fall off track and always have the opportunity to get back on track, which feels energizing and renewing. View your relationship with your goals as an ongoing journey where you grow through the variety of ups and downs you will encounter along the way.

As we have heard often, "It's not necessarily about the goal, it's about who you become along the way to reaching the goal."

It's faulty thinking to expect that setting goals once will keep you on track and get you there. You will need multiple opportunities to review and adjust your goals. You will need to make them feel fresh along the way. You will need to keep your relationship with your goals alive and passionate. Yes, it's a lot like dating your goals. Keep the interest alive. Keep pursuing. Keep the romance. Don't let them get away!

Five tips to make REACHING YOUR GOALS easier.

ONE: Always be thinking of the next action step you can take toward your goal. Large or small. When you establish the mindset that you are consistently acting toward your goal, the momentum naturally takes off. You see milestone after milestone of results and you naturally believe you are getting there. Feels good!

TWO: Write your goals on something to carry with you at all times. Keeping your goals with you is a powerful way to integrate them into your consciousness. As the goals guru might say, "Be at One with Your Goals!"

THREE: Schedule time to review your goals. Make it a priority to get your goal list out and work with it. Still feel current? Need to add anything? Action steps established? Make it a regular part of your schedule.

FOUR: Visualize the achievement of your goals. If you are a visual person, collect images that represent the feelings of achieving each goal. If you are a word person, keep a journal or poster containing words that activate your feelings of accomplishment. The emotional experience of manifesting our goals is the most significant factor in being able to reach them.

FIVE: Be persistent. Do something that represents your goals every day. Expand your thinking to include things you've never done before, because I bet you have never committed to doing

SOMETHING every day that moves you toward your goals. This act alone can be your game-changer. This act alone can be the #1 reason that you actually achieve your goals this year. What if you recorded a statement into your phone or sent yourself and email EVERY DAY about your goals? Make a simple a statement or renewed commitment – the point is in the action, not the content of your statement.

EXERCISES

GET GUMPTION

Write one goal or one tip on a small card to keep in your wallet. Take it out and read it every time you open your wallet.

JOURNAL THIS:

- ◊ How do you acknowledge yourself? Success Author Brian Tracy writes, *"You are completely responsible for everything you are today, for everything you think, say and do, and for everything you become from this moment forward."* What does this mean to YOU?

- ◊ List three things you have completed recently? Note the positive momentum you created with each completion and write down how it benefits the people in your life.

GET UNPLUGGED

Growing through the variety of ups and downs is like riding a wave in the ocean. The higher the wave, the deeper the wake that follows it. The wisdom is in enjoying the peak while it lasts and enjoy the valley when it comes. The high point is excitement, and the low point is relaxation. Take some time to notice that we do not exist permanently in either one.

MEDITATE THIS:

- "This too shall pass."
- Imagine you are riding a wave, riding a tiger or riding a rollercoaster. Imagine celebrating every moment of the ride.

13

Are You a Control Freak?

Control isn't always a bad thing. Learning to control the things we DO have control over (Example: Ourselves!) is a great addition to confidence and self-esteem. You and I both know that trying to control others does not work.

We are ALL Control Freaks in some area of our lives, at different times, and we always have the opportunity to notice it, catch ourselves and choose to either let go or focus on improving OURSELVES instead.

Seven Signs You Are a Control Freak

1. You try to change the thoughts, words or actions of others because you know you are right.
2. You criticize, give advice or give your opinion when you are not asked.
3. You interrupt.
4. You need things to go your way or you are not interested.
5. You are frustrated. (Daily frustration is a huge neon sign that you are trying to control something.)
6. You micromanage or present scenarios that advance your own agenda.
7. You just have to know. You feel the need to have all the answers before you can move forward.

I found myself in several of these, as I'm sure you did too. My first clue was the thought that my mother is a pro at every single one of these signs. Stop! I'm projecting onto my mother. How about, "Where am I the pro?" So. . . . are you wanting to copy this page to "show it to someone else?" Busted! Own your inner control freak.

Notice if you recognize any of these thoughts:

"If I don't improve my career I'm a failure." "If I don't get this contract I'm going to fall apart." "If I can't be positive every day with my kids I'm a terrible parent." "If I don't feel comfortable I can't go." The stress in our lives makes it easy to get stuck in irrational thoughts. Then the sabotage kicks in and we attempt to control the situation, usually by trying to control other people.

Control Freaks never see their controlling behaviors as symptoms of what's really happening because their anxiety has sky-rocketed and blocks a clear perspective. Their unwillingness to accept a specific situation has ignited their fear.

A Control Freak anticipates an outcome they think is unacceptable which holds them in a fear-based panic.

You can easily let go of controlling behaviors when you work on getting in touch with what really IS going on. The idea that "controlling the situation" will make it better is an absolute joke. It's been proven over and over again in Life that attempts at controlling things NEVER succeed. Is a situational triumph more important than a full-picture victory of lasting value?

There is a "Control Freak" inside of every one of us. The gift of our controlling nature is found in the qualities of determination, focus, and desire for well-being. These qualities are underneath every controlling choice we make. We need to make room for these qualities to get expressed directly and in the light.

Can you embrace controlling part of yourself with non-judgment?

If you can allow your "inner control freak" to take the back seat rather than the driver's seat, you can enjoy the ride much more.

The first step to overcome controlling behaviors is being able to identify where the seven signs show up in your life. Maybe you see all seven. Maybe you see one or two.

Six ways to overcome controlling behaviors:

1. Check your expectations of others. Are they realistic? If not, let them go!

2. Quit the passive-aggressive nonsense and BE DIRECT!

3. Accept that much of life falls into the category called, "The Unknown."

4. Embrace confrontation--it is often the best thing you can do.

5. Take charge of your own happiness. Say YES to being responsible for the happy you.

6. Be vulnerable with people. If you don't like the word "vulnerable" - just be more genuine or more transparent or more open.

Put a stop to your controlling behaviors, and instead become a better version of yourself.

EXERCISES

GET GUMPTION

Have two conversations this week:

What do you expect from your family members?

What do you expect from your partner/lover?

JOURNAL THIS:

- ◊ Write down the "Six ways to overcome controlling behaviors." Commit to following them for 3 weeks. Track your results.
- ◊ Choose your personal "top three" ways.

GET UNPLUGGED

Use your sensual side to move with the rhythms of nature. In this way you radiate the peace within you, and it's easier to let your spirit be free. Control is the obsession of your fear-based small minded thinking. Access your spirit instead.

MEDITATE THIS:

- ◊ My eyes close into the soft velvety unknown, and I love feeling comfortable there.
- ◊ My body is a lake and I can move freely like water, slowly and beautifully, from the inside out.

14

Are You Emotionally Available?

We all have experienced a relationship with an emotionally unavailable person at some point in our lives. Some people sadly know nothing else. Some people recognize this early, learn their lessons and move on to healthy connections. If you use Google to search "emotionally unavailable" you will find an abundance of information and resources.

The key to understanding emotional unavailability is that the person who is unavailable doesn't want love as much as they want control. They believe emotions are unsafe. Feeling "in control" gives them a sense of safety.

"Emotional Unavailability" is the inability of one person to reach out and make a heart connection to another person.

I used to think that an emotionally unavailable person just needed to be fixed or taught or inspired in the right way. Now I understand that these people are simply unable to connect emotionally. Accepting that is freedom.

What about looking within ourselves? Where would you rate yourself in the area of Self Care? Are you nurturing your own emotions? There are many ways we can take care of ourselves emotionally. By taking 100% responsibility for our own well-being (especially when it comes to matters of the heart) we have a much greater chance at emotionally fulfilling connections and relationships.

When someone else turns out NOT to be making an emotional connection with you, it causes trauma. The trauma is painful. This undermines your expectations of yourself and your abilities to make connections. Take notice of this and allow it to fill you with determination to support your own emotional strength.

The more you can be aware of your emotional well-being, the less prone you are to falling into an unsatisfying (or worse) connection with someone else.

When I help my clients "get unstuck", we look for patterns or perspectives to move forward instead. I ask them, "What are you getting out of that?" as a way to illuminate choices that are keeping them stuck.

Three perspectives on why you keep repeating negative patterns around emotional unavailability:

ONE: You love the fantasy of being able to fix or change another person.

How exciting is it to feel powerful? How much adrenaline do you get to produce by anticipating, or expecting, or orchestrating or manipulating? Can be such a thrill, however, check clearly with yourself after the adrenaline rush subsides. You are left feeling empty and full of doubt. Your self-esteem is puddled on the floor, and now you get to be a superhero and pick yourself up once again. Just look at how amazing you are to survive, or even make it look like you can thrive, in such a drama-infused scenario. It's exhausting, isn't it?

TWO: You think that your LOVE will create a positive outcome or a transformation.

Is it time to face your inflated ego? Ask yourself if you can even know that it's true. Can your love really transform an unavailable person?

You cannot know it's true. What is possible instead if you channel all that love back into yourself?? Much more. So very much more.

THREE: You are addicted to hoping rather than comfortable with the reality of acceptance.

What are you really waiting for? This false happiness or excitement is just taking you out of the present moment and pushing you into a pretend future where you live happily ever after. Today looks different. Today hold the truth where you would absolutely make a change and move on. Figure out how to support yourself in order to act from the present. The present is truth. Your future fantasy doesn't exist.

Waiting for someone to "come around" gives you the chance to feel giving, or patient, or amazing or some other quality you are attracted to.

Here's the truth. You must be willing to give those qualities to yourself FIRST, without going indirectly through a dysfunctional pattern to ignite them in yourself. This makes it an inauthentic experience and you can only add further dysfunction on top of it. Back up, start at the source of your own truth.

It's natural to think that by fixing this "out there" with the other person, you will find healing or peace.

The best approach is to look first at the opportunity the other person is giving YOU to take responsibility for your own emotional wellbeing.

They are simply reminding you to take charge of your worth and desire to connect emotionally to others. Yes, an unavailable person can be your greatest teacher. Just hand them an apple and a thank you note, and move on to a healthy person who can connect with you openly and directly.

EXERCISES

GET GUMPTION

Pick a quality you most want to express (Examples: Giving, Confident, Supportive, Loving) and write the quality on post-it notes so you can see it in several locations. Act out this quality in everything you do on a daily basis.

JOURNAL THIS:

- ◊ List two thoughts about being vulnerable. Write down one reason for each about why this holds you back.
- ◊ Now, write a note to each thought or reasons thanking them for serving you (or doing you a favor of some kind.)

GET UNPLUGGED

Imagine the illusion of control as a veil of thin ice that looks shimmery and attractive at first glance. It will shatter or melt away instantly when the light shines beneath – demonstrating again how fragile and unreliable this ILLUSION really is.

MEDITATE THIS:

- ◊ Fulfillment is wealth on all levels.
- ◊ There is much more to life than being "on top of things."

15

Can you Change a Naysayer into a Supporter?

When the people around you are negative it can really weigh you down. Sometimes our relationships hit a groove where we might not notice the negativity. The dictionary definition of "Naysayer" is person who habitually expresses negative or pessimistic views.

Scan through your relationships with your spouse, boyfriend/girlfriend, co-workers or friends/family. Are you experiencing criticisms or disrespect of any kind? Is anyone or anything trying to stop you from being fully expressed or successful where you want to be? If your friends or loved ones are keeping you from "going for it" or giving something the time and energy it needs, then it's time for you to transform the negativity. What if you could even turn them into powerful supporters of you and your dreams?

It's important to remember that most people do not intend to be hurtful, negative or mean. It's highly likely they are driven by something fearful and are unaware of it's power over them.

People who are "Naysayers" take the role of questioning or limiting an idea or goal even when they feel positive toward it underneath their comments or behavior. Stop giving the Naysayers in your life credit and instead take charge of how you respond to them.

Transform a Naysayer by addressing three key issues:

ONE:

Are they afraid of something? Address the fear rather than their negativity.

If you are doing something new or pursuing a goal in any area, people in your life might have one or more of the following fears:

If you become successful, you would not have time for them.

If you become successful, they will feel jealous or abandoned in some way.

If you try and fail, they will suffer somehow as a result.

If you become successful, they will feel less about themselves, or feel bad for underachieving.

TWO:

What is your own "stuff" that causes you to attract negativity into your life?

How are YOU causing most of the negativity you are experiencing? Look at beliefs like, "I don't deserve this" or "Success is going to be hard". These type of beliefs trigger insecure or unprocessed emotions and we are likely to project them onto others which ends up looking like they are being negative. A negative dynamic can transform instantly just by YOU showing up differently.

THREE:

Examine your comfort level with CHANGE.

Even though we fully embrace a new goal or desire, we forget to be compassionate about the anxiety and fear that comes with making big changes. Remember that you are a creature of comfort and that you need to take care of yourself in the midst of risking and changing and growing. Not paying attention to your vulnerability in this area costs you negativity in your relationships. Can you really afford to be around a Naysayer?

Handle your fear and anxiety levels by taking one step at a time and by feeding the flame of your relationships with authenticity and open heart.

EXERCISES

Follow these six tips to help with the transformation:

1. Ask for help regarding your goals/vision.
2. Let people know your dream, and your "WHY".
3. Own your fears – take responsibility for your emotions and energy.
4. Take charge by having a plan in place. (Specific and clear for each step)
5. Set boundaries for your privacy and self-care.
6. Only communicate with others who have earned your trust.

When you communicate with a naysayer, it's important to eliminate your defensiveness. Being defensive about your desires or passion keeps you from being calm, peaceful and rational when discussing your position. Do whatever you need to feel detached so you can express the rational side of your passions.

16

Will You LISTEN to Me?

Hear me. Get what I'm saying. Understand me. This is the short list of how most of us want to feel. Being a good listener is a powerful tool. Let's take it out of the toolbox and create more success in our personal and professional lives.

When we are feeling heard, understood and have a sense of connection, we are much happier. We feel more grounded, more at ease, and we get the sense that we are in line with goodness. Why would you NOT want to cultivate that in someone you are talking with? And yes, I said talking "with". Think of someone who talks and talks AT you. Are you looking frantically for the nearest exit?

A conversation about Listening has two components: The skills and the strategy. This statement deepened my commitment to being a good listener: **Listening is the Most Benevolent Act.**

It's true that listening is giving. Listening is being of service. If I want to give first, all I have to do is listen well. This is the law of reciprocity.

Maybe this feels counterproductive to your usual approach to life or business, especially when you want to get something done, or achieve something specific. This is a perfect time to shift into a giving or serving stance instead because you are probably attached to your own agenda or expected outcome, and quite frankly, you will get a lesser result than is possible when you expand into giving or service.

Think about what keeps you from listening well. The biggest sabotage I see in my work with people, is simply not trusting. Ask yourself if you are afraid that you will lose out on something. The truth is that "you will get your chance". Don't let the urgency or panic of needing to get your turn or get your word in be the culprit of listening instead.

You must trust that being the listener gives you everything to gain. When you see it this way, you are able to practice some higher awareness skills such as "Trusting the Process" and "Trusting in Positive Outcomes".

If your intention is to "deeply listen" you can begin to see ways to help, or offer, or assist, or provide, or contribute . . . these are all powerful qualities to cultivate. A good listener is always asking themselves, "What am I observing that I can ask about?"

Want to be more powerful in your relationship? LISTEN.

Imagine that the more you deposit with a person, the more valuable you are to that person. The more you have on account with them, the easier it is to make a withdrawal when needed. Your objective is to create a surplus of wealth in the relationship by depositing as much as possible. **Your currency is LISTENING!** Invest your currency wisely.

You can implement better listening right away, without studying listening techniques or learning new skills. Are you willing to shift? Simply make a commitment to "Listen Better Now." Those are influential words. Demonstrating this commitment can be easy.

Imagine that you set an intention for every conversation that included three simple things:

     1.   **To connect.**
     2.   **To find the gift.**
     3.   **To experience the greatest outcome for ALL.**

We all share a desire for these things. Take leadership to offer it first, and the benefits of more joy and more success will ultimately follow for all involved. That's just how it works.

Four habits to make you a masterful listener:

Cultivate these habits, and your listening skills will naturally improve and shine.

First, Be Present.

Be in the moment and fully aware of what's happening. Your energy is supportive and your nature is flexible. Put your gadgets and screens away. Leave your residual stress at the door.

Second, Reach Out.

Be in the receiving rather than the delivering. Create dialog, not monolog. Your energy is authentic and genuine. Imagine your heart opening and hold that position. Your nature is open and inviting.

Third, Be Naturally Expressive

Your emotions are free flowing and unedited. Your body language is open and congruent. There is no editing, no game-face. Your nature is simply and easily expressed.

Fourth, Cultivate Self Understanding

Your Self-awareness is strong and you have a sense of self-acceptance, wisdom and integrity. Your personal passion is vibrant. Your nature is grounded and at peace.

17

Am I Feeling Intimidated?

Do you catch yourself thinking that someone is "above you"?

Or that you are "not enough"?

How many times have you stopped yourself by thinking that someone is looking down on you? No-one can intimidate you without your permission. Live your life with heart and never doubt your value.

When you feel intimidated, do you make an assumption about the attitude or authority of your intimidator? Are you judging?

We naturally make snap-judgments or assumptions about others, but how can we know that any of it is true? Remind yourself that you really do NOT know if it's true, and you will set yourself free from the perceived intimidation.

If you do not make the effort to confirm your assumptions about someone, you are blocking your opportunity to engage with them confidently. You block the chance to create a relationship that could ultimately benefit you (and them.)

According to Wikipedia, intimidation is intentional behavior that "would cause a person of ordinary sensibilities" fear of injury or harm. Intimidation can be delivered to others externally, and it can be received and experienced on a personal level or internally.

To make our lives more successful and more peaceful, let's eliminate the stuck place of being intimidated by anyone or anything. At its full potential, intimidation is a catalyst to take action. The same way we can use anger in a healthy way to channel our actions toward a positive resolve.

Feeling intimated brings out the emotions of frustration, envy, fear, self-doubt, and all versions of negative feelings. Taking steps to even the playing field, or eliminate the wrong perspective brings out emotions related to positive feelings. Imagine feeling free to respond to anyone or anything from an authentically present and confident position. You are feeling radiant, open, creative, willing, and full of sweet anticipation. Now it's clear to see the value in overcoming intimidation.

What intimidation feel like? Probably a fearful anticipation of injury or harm. Notice what your fear is about when you feel intimidated. Do you fear rejection? Do you fear humiliation? Do you fear being discovered as a fraud? Do you fear feeling that you are not enough? Fear of a loss?

When someone's behavior causes us to feel intimidated, we can notice our fear and then make a choice to handle it.

The first step to freedom of intimidation is to recognize that your experience is about the fear that is triggered and NOT about the person's behavior.

If you make your experience about "how terribly intimidating that person is being", you have skipped the opportunity to take charge of your fears and your ability to overcome them so that you can be free of intimidation forever.

This work is simple. I'm not saying it's easy, but it is very simple when you see it step by step. The gift is in the huge payoff of freedom and increased confidence.

Five steps to move beyond intimidation and feel powerful.

Step one, notice your fearful feelings.

Step two, validate your assumptions about the situation or person.

Step three, take ownership that it's your own personal choice to feel intimidated.

Step four, look for ways to let go of your fear or other negative feelings that got triggered in the situation.

Step five, step back into the situation with confidence, curiosity, and positive intentions.

Intimidation has us feeling afraid or timid. Overcoming intimidation is about overcoming a communication that makes you afraid to try something. What makes you feel timid?

When you feel intimidated, what kind of choices do you make?

What kind of choices would you make in the absence of intimidation?

Three ways to self-coach out of feeling intimidated:

One: Write down a few qualities that you could purposely express in order to overcome an intimidating situation. An example might be determination, or gumption or confidence. Choose the top two qualities. Next time you feel intimidated, consciously choose to fully express those qualities, or to talk to yourself about those qualities so that you can shift the experience immediately.

Two: Look at any situation where you feel intimidated, and wave the magic wand to erase anything related to intimidation. Now answer this question, "What would you DO or SAY instead?"

Three: Imagine that you have a portable pedestal. It automatically inflates any time you want to use it. You can place yourself on it, or you can place someone else on it. It's YOUR choice. You can now look at any exchange from a different perspective depending on where you place the pedestal. Now you notice the pedestal has an expansion button. Make room for everyone on the same pedestal. It's even. It's a foundation of equality.

18

Can You "Hold the Space" for Someone?

Imagine an experience of support that feels solid and completely unlimited. Think of a time when you felt supported and held in your greatest expression. If someone was holding a space for you to be or do whatever was in your best interest, would you feel uplifted? Supported? Would you feel present to your best abilities?

The act of truly being with another person in this way is what I call, "Holding the Space."

I work with my clients in ways that brings out their best. We need to do more of this for each other. We must learn these skills and commit to sharing them regularly.

I encourage "holding the space" in every opportunity we have because it is such a profound act of service. It makes huge impact. It creates meaning and allows room for big results.

One client was challenged in her relationship with her adult daughter. She was resisting and fighting for control and putting a lot of energy into avoiding her fears, and when I invited her to simply "hold the space" for her daughter to come around in her own time you would have thought the burning bush appeared or that the bluebirds started singing under cleared skies. Such a beautiful shift. She can still take action, but imagine the different choices she makes based on holding the space FOR her daughter rather than being absorbed in her own space of neediness, fear and control.

Holding the space means letting go of everything except your commitment to the greatest expression possible in the moment.

Holding the space is best achieved with an understanding that everything is energy. Having a positive mindset and seeing positive outcomes are actions that create positive energy. It's easy to hold the space for someone when you are committed to their positive outcome. (Remember not to be attached to what YOU think their outcome should be.)

You can influence experiences by showing up in a commitment to positive energy. This can be a very new or confusing idea if you are not used to this perspective. I bet that when you close your eyes and go inside to ask yourself "Am I committed to positive energy right now?" that you will have a clear knowing.

Start simple and let yourself grow into a greater understanding of how you can be of service by "holding space for others".

Can you hold the space for your lover to "just be" or to deal with it in their own time?

Can you hold the space for someone you love to make a mess or stumble or whatever they may need to do in order to arrive at their destination with clarity and wisdom?

Can you hold the space for your family to love each other?

Can you hold the space for yourself?

Can you hold the space for a dear friend who is taking a huge risk and wanting to do her very best?

What if holding the space for someone is your only choice. It would mean setting your own agenda aside and opening up to the highest good or right action for THEM. What a powerful practice of love and service. If you are familiar with prayer or if you have a strong spiritual practice, you are already holding space.

Prayer creates a space for guidance, receiving, balancing, connecting and love. These are all components of holding space.

Give someone an experience of themselves that is guided by their greater self. Give them an experience where they can receive, balance and connect to the absolute LOVE that flows all around them, making all things possible.

How can you hold a space somewhere that matters to you?

> **Teachers hold a space for their student's success.**
>
> **Generous lovers hold a space for each other's fulfillment and highest pleasure.**
>
> **Parents hold a space for their kid's to grow.**
>
> **Leaders hold a space for growth and inspiration.**

Start today by holding the space for your own receiving. Allow more acknowledgment of your gifts and accomplishments. Allow yourself to bask in your own LOVE.

19

Uplifting Self-Talk Tips

Make sure you listen carefully to the way you talk to yourself. Discover how much time you spend criticizing or beating yourself up to notice huge opportunities for positive change. Imagine you are holding an adorable teddy bear. Every hour you call it names or remind it how much better things could have gone, or tell it negative statements about shortcomings, lack or never being enough. Isn't it ironic to expect this precious teddy bear to relax and enjoy "life"? You expect it to take care of others? To easily be love and give love? And yet. . . . We do this type of damage to ourselves frequently. We diminish our potential and our unique contribution to the world. Ouch!

It's 100% possible to replace negative self-talk with something gentler, motivating, acknowledging and uplifting. Transforming the way we talk to ourselves on this journey is a top priority. It's our human nature to seek personal growth, whether emotionally, financially, mentally or spiritually.

Improving your self-talk is the key to taking actions that bring great rewards.

How often have you heard this quote or something similar? "Change your thoughts, change your life." Or, "Change the way you think, and automatically change the results you get in your life." Let's handle it at the foundation by changing the way you talk to yourself.

Now is your chance to catch negative talk in action and STOP. Awareness is the key. If you are blocked or struggling with finding your own thoughts, use traditional tools like journaling or prayer or a conversation with a trusted person who can help you explore. Contact me for a 3-step process to help you access your internal dialogue. There are many options so you can initiate changes right away.

Four self-talk tips to use immediately:

Keep in mind these tips are useless unless you sincerely have the intent to become a positive thinker.

ONE: Eliminate Downer Chat

Notice statements like, "I can't" or "Not me". Notice if you are still listening to old stories about something you did wrong or something someone told you was wrong. Look for the classic, "I'm not smart enough, or good enough." Listen for "I don't have what it takes" which can come in several versions.

These statements create resistance which will sabotage any attempt you are making at positive growth or change. Simply cancel out ANY negative internal input. Imagine holding up an internal STOP SIGN when you notice the downer chat happening. Visualize it's disappearance.

TWO: Lock Into Positive Affirmations

Make a simple statement about something you believe or something you want to achieve. You must take complete responsibility to use one that feels absolutely true to you. If your affirmation elicits even the smallest bit of doubt in the back of your mind, it will not be effective. For example, if you want a loving committed relationship, instead of saying, "I am in a loving committed relationship!" you can say instead, "I love knowing that I am creating a loving committed relationship!" Add words that make room for the process. Make room to believe it.

Expand your affirmations in ways that allow you to feel confident about attracting what you want. When you create a positive flow with yourself, there is no room to make yourself wrong or attack yourself. This type of transformation makes positive results happen naturally.

THREE: Focus on Enjoyable Moments:

Positive self-talk thrives when you are focusing on positive images and thoughts. Fill your awareness with gratitude for what you have presently. Tell yourself stories about joyful experiences. Include ways you can acknowledge yourself as well. Your self-talk will automatically change to be in alignment with the joy you are creating inside of yourself.

Keep a gratitude list on your smart phone or in a notebook.

FOUR: Extinguish Negative Influences:

Do a simple inventory of where you encounter negativity with other people, other situations, or choices you regularly make. Choosing to be around positive people who inspire you is much more powerful than navigating the challenges of being around negative people. What stories, television shows or reading materials do you choose? Are any of them negative or a source of negative self-talk for you? What conversations do you choose or initiate? Eliminate anything that extinguishes your positive flame. Fuel yourself with the opposite so your internal flame can burn brightly. Make positive self-talk your priority.

It's realistic to expect that replacing negative self-talk with more positive input will take some work and time.

You will feel empowered and your inner teddy bear will gift the world with positivity and fulfillment.

20

Do You Wait Until the Last Minute?

Every area of our lives includes opportunities to plan ahead. At work and at home, life is full of anticipation for things. Do you wait until the last minute to get ready? Do you wait until the night before or the day before? It's human nature to procrastinate.

Planning ahead is a valuable skill we can learn, and is a process we can continue perfecting. AND, learning how to embrace the gift of last minute action is also a valuable skill.

I invite you to see this part of life differently. What if doing preparation at the last minute is positive and beneficial? What if the choice to get ready for something right before it happens creates even better results? So often we agonizing over not being prepared for something we care about. We beat ourselves up for procrastinating or not having enough time. When we look at the situation objectively, it's usually evident that there really wasn't time available previously. Next we beat ourselves up for approaching something "wrong" when in reality we are in a positive and productive flow.

We are taught in life that being prepared ahead of time is a good and valiant way to be. This is true. However, when life is full, busy and unpredictable, and timing turns out to be condensed, we need to be free to choose a "last minute" preparation without judging ourselves as falling short or doing it wrong.

Change your mindset from "if only I had more time to prepare" into "the time I have to prepare is enough", and the outcome is always positive.

What needs to be in place when you are preparing at the last minute so that it is productive and even ENJOYABLE? What do you need to feel confident and in control so that when the event happens you know you did your best and can feel positive about it?

The power we have when we make ourselves wrong is huge. The added stress and negativity is 100% up to us. Look clearly at your choices and take responsibility for working with what you have, rather than beating yourself up for "not doing it the way you should. . .. "

Most often, the feeling of falling short is based on how you made yourself feel rather than the actual outcome. My favorite quote by Maya Angelou is powerful when we apply it to OURSELVES.

> "People don't remember what you said or what you did. They remember how you made them feel." -Maya Angelou

Now re-frame this when you are preparing at the last minute, "I will remember how I made ME feel. . ." and use that truth to set yourself up for success.

Avoid at all costs any tendency to make yourself wrong. Instead, take on the energy of seeing your timeline as a positive. How FUN to be in a situation where you can perform at your fullest? How FUN to pull out the stops and use your resources to make something happen? How FUN to set yourself up for a wild adventure. How FUN to discover what happens.

Your perspective can be one of excitement if you decide to free yourself of "shoulds" and limiting self-criticism. When those things are out of the way, you make room for the thrill of your spontaneity and experiencing your potential.

The key component to overcoming the trap of making yourself wrong is to notice if you are using the situation to activate a deeper story that keeps you stuck. For example, do you always find yourself singing the "I'm not good enough" song? Procrastinating can be used as a perfect activation for this song to come out. Notice this, and your awareness already gives you the freedom to choose differently.

If you fall into the rut of "fear of failing", it's imperative that you notice how you use that story to make yourself wrong for procrastinating. What if instead, you used the power and adrenaline that occurs the night before to keep your focus and commitment to performing at the top of your game? And when you do, take the time to celebrate yourself. How would you talk to yourself if you believed in YOU? If you were your own best cheerleader?

Acknowledge yourself for the amazing qualities you were able to bring forth and take responsibility for the positive parts of what you were able to do. Make this process your new best friend. If life throws you a curve ball, (and that is guaranteed!) take it on with gumption and be sure you allow only positive communication with yourself during the process. See it through to doing your best and whoop it up afterward.

SECTION THREE:
Broaden Your Horizons

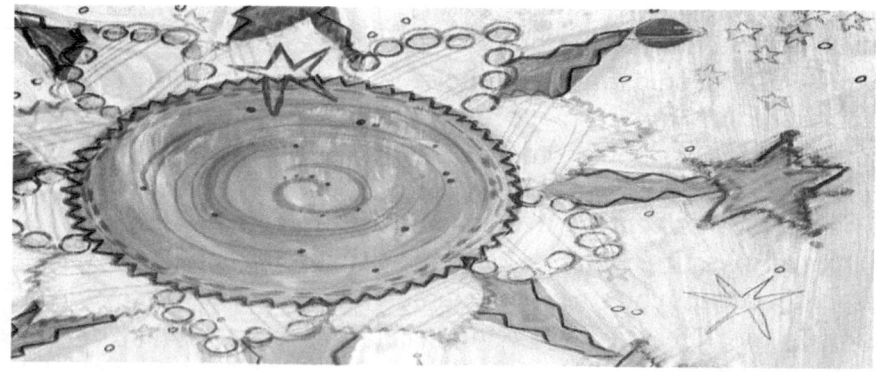

"Discovery consists not in seeking new lands, but in seeing with new eyes."

—Marcel Proust

THIS SECTION INCLUDES POINTS OF VIEW TO HELP YOU:

- ✓ Slow down and get more done. (With JOY!)
- ✓ Give and receive opportunities to connect.
- ✓ Celebrate your self-worth more and more.
- ✓ Know that you are wealthy beyond measure.
- ✓ Get unstuck quicker each time you slip.
- ✓ Be flexible and comfortable managing your attention.
- ✓ Create richness and more meaning in your life.
- ✓ Enjoy the balance of thinking and feeling.
- ✓ Be comfortable listening to confrontation or criticism.
- ✓ Be open and curious rather than righteous.

21

Can My Life Be Easy?

Do you often push yourself and try to move too fast? Why do we believe that doing more things and doing them faster and faster is the better accomplishment?

A powerful question you can ask yourself in every area of your life is this: "What if this is going to be EASY?" This instantly makes room for appreciation and even gratitude for what you do or experience.

Author Karl Palachuk writes in his book, "Relax, Focus, Succeed" about the power of slowing down to get more done.

Karl teaches us to focus on one high priority task at a time and stop trying to multi-task which is only an illusion of productivity.

Moving too fast causes us to experience stress, anxiety and distraction. By "taking it easy" you can stop and create a different experience right away. IF it is easy, then it makes sense to relax, breathe, trust and know that everything is working out.

Take it easy? Best reminder of all time.

Notice if you focus on moving fast and trying to get as much done as possible. Most often it's just an illusion that you are working hard and getting more things done, but it's usually the opposite. When you move slower you often get more done, because you take the time to do things right the first time. Having to go back and correct mistakes, or getting burned out because you are pushing too hard is costly to your time, productivity and life balance.

Be aware of your choices to move fast or push through something, and give yourself room to choose an easier approach which will create a much more positive outcome.

Four choices to create new habits:

Be deliberate and mindful. Slow yourself down physically. Choose to make your movements slower. It's fun to practice this skill by "mindful eating." What if you ate a piece of fruit in the slowest way possible? Practice chewing slowly, breathing between bites, savoring flavors. All the benefits you discover in this practice are transferable to everything you do elsewhere in your life.

Focus on doing one thing at a time. Do you feel depleted when you do too much and make mistakes? Cherish and protect your mental resources by "taking it easy" one step at a time.

Eliminate as many distractions as you possibly can. Would it serve your well-being to work by yourself where others can't bother you? Or can you get away from technology, phones or TV? What would make your environment more peaceful?

Stop and reflect. Did you do everything the way you wanted to? Do you feel content with your present completion? You can make it a habit to ask yourself, "Do I feel complete? Or do I need anything else before I move on to the next thing?"

A common challenge in our daily lives is taking time to do things consciously and to allow for more enjoyment by moving slower. If you have made commitments and set boundaries for this part of your life, give yourself a round of applause!

Do you notice any resistance as you read these suggestions? Are you fearful that "taking it easy" will sabotage you in some way? Are you wondering if it really matters? These are all reasonable concerns, and until you take the risk of changing behaviors or choices, you will never know what is possible.

EXERCISES

GET GUMPTION

Divide a sheet of paper into two columns: "Old Hard Way" and "New Easy Way". Select the next activity or project you have coming up and describe your plan in each column.

JOURNAL THIS:

- ◊ What are five activities I do in my life that could be easier?
- ◊ Write yourself a love note giving yourself permission to take it easy. Apologize for being hard on yourself.

GET UNPLUGGED

There is no need to do anything but rest in the fullness of who you are right now. Savor this quality of slowing down, of coming to rest and recognizing that you are already exactly where you need to be.

MEDITATE THIS:

- ◊ My essence is at ease. Hold a flower or leaf and meditate on this thought: "My essence is at ease."
- ◊ Look at an image or a scene from nature. Ask it to show you what can be easier.

22

Do You Love Being Asked "A Good Question?"

Does it feel good to anticipate something useful and enlightening? Recall the last time you were asked something that made you stop and think about yourself. When this happens to me I experience a bristle of excitement because I know I'm going to learn something about myself. I also feel the sweet tingle that someone is caring enough to ASK. Those good feelings are priceless.

What if you made it your intention to give this kind of experience to the people you care about? Asking questions that demonstrate your true curiosity is a huge gift. You are showing the other person a treasure chest of things we value most in life: love, compassion, being present, connection and supporting each other's growth. So valuable and so easy to do.

When someone asks you a question that makes you stop and think, the floodgates of possibility open wide. You have just entered the connection to your greater self. Maybe you'll want to throw your arms around that person and shower them with gratitude for creating this experience for you. Or simply, and more subtly, you may want to let them watch the opening of your heart as you answer. Such a lovely gift.

Top three benefits of "A Good Question!"

ONE: I get to learn about myself.

Seems there is a shortage of opportunities for this most cherished aspect of being human. Our world is too busy and cluttered with distractions and we need to mindfully take time to honor our own precious evolution. We thrive when we learn, we adore the chance to grow in self-awareness.

TWO: I get to notice what lights me up.

Looking at ourselves from a suggested perspective is great practice to own our motivations. Clients come to me all the time wanting to understand their purpose or wanting to find more motivation. This feeling of "a good question!" gives us an instant spotlight for clarity. The feeling of "wow, that's a good question!" shows you something new that grabs your attention in a powerful way, and is likely to indicate your core passions. Bring out what lights you up, and you now have the choice to take action at a deeper level.

THREE: I get to think in a different way.

Maybe what you really feel is "thank you for busting me out of my cage!" Our thought patterns become old and tired and we get stuck. A needed boost feels refreshing and freeing. The curious personal question that is delivered just at the right time gives you a burst of light on a whole new perspective. Quite exciting indeed.

Good questions are the gift that keeps on giving. When you activate positive feelings in another person, you are depositing directly into the wealth of your relationship with them. The bank account between you grows and you can draw on it at any time. The currency you deposit is listening, curiosity and genuine love for the soul of the other person. A beautiful exchange.

The experience of receiving a "good question" is loaded with the sense of growth. Growing makes life exciting.

Here are some ideas and tools for asking "good questions" so that you can give this gift easily. What makes a "good question?" It must be an authentically delivered curiosity about what would move the other person forward.

Ask a "good question" by **first asking yourself** a few good questions:

What really matters here?
What can I be curious about?
What does my intuition want me to ask?
What would they be saying if their inner superhero was talking?
Then, ask them a question FROM that reference point in yourself. Yes, it may feel awkward at first, but I guarantee that when you practice the art of asking good questions, you will master it sooner than you think.

Three questions to elicit the response, "Wow! That's a good question!"

"If you had no fear, what would you do?"

"What would happen if you took the next step now?"

"Are you thinking forward or are you thinking backward right now?"

There are multiple angles and opportunities to ask questions and every situation is unique. The main idea is to be curious. Let your fully expressed life unfold from the center of curiosity.

EXERCISES

GET GUMPTION

Meet with someone you are curious about and ask them three *good questions.*

JOURNAL THIS:

- ◊ What are three "good questions" you would like to be asked?
- ◊ List your top two favorite conversation topics. How can you ask others about these topics?

GET UNPLUGGED

Curiosity activates your natural ability to listen from your heart and your inner wisdom. Our biology is naturally curious. When two people are fully present with each other, curiosity comes easily and exploring it can be a great way to celebrate feelings of discovery and connection.

MEDITATE THIS:

- ◊ My inner world is naturally curious and filled with nourishing discoveries.
- ◊ My curious energy connects me to bigger and better things all the time.

23

How Do You Get Past Self Doubt?

The culprit to our satisfaction in life is always connected to how we value ourselves. The belief that somehow or somewhere we are "NOT ENOUGH" is the main block to our fulfillment.

When is the last time you had an opportunity to do something and you hesitated or resisted? Your excuses probably fell into this category, "I'm not ready. I don't know what to do. I doubt I could...."

Notice that these excuses amplify the message of, "I'm not smart enough. Or I'm not good enough. Or I should be better *something*, in order to say yes to this opportunity with confidence and gumption.

We all face the obstacle of not valuing our own gifts and worth in many different areas of our life. Getting over it produces a big glowing sense of freedom.

What does it take to move forward with increased self-worth when you are underneath the wet blanket of self-doubt?

Four tips to eliminate self-doubt.

ONE: Look at the situation before you and find where you can feel the most excited about it. If you find a place to get excited, the positive perspective will create good energy naturally. In other words, eliminate the areas where you feel stopped or overwhelmed about the situation and instead find one small part of it you can at least *begin to feel* excited. Now you have a starting place.

TWO: Choose simplicity. The main reason most of my clients plummet into the dregs of self-doubt is overwhelm resulting from making the scenario much bigger than it really is.

THREE: Do not buy into the self-sabotaging thought that you are NOT ENOUGH. This belief creates a state where we constantly need to fill something. Or replace or adjust or improve. All that energy is about going backwards and compensating for an absence. Imagine the stark contrast to shifting your energy into going forward and doing the opposite, which is to create from the abundance of what IS already enough.

Ask yourself a powerful question in your daily life. "Am I filling emptiness or am I creating forward momentum with what already is enough?"

Our main challenge with this is our perception. Work your positive mindset as if it's a muscle you can flex and build so that it keeps getting easier and easier to KNOW you are a high worth being, with incredible value.

FOUR: Notice who benefits when you own your worth. Who is touched in a good way when you remember your value? Look around your community of loved ones, friends and people in your life. Who are you depriving by not being confident of your gifts? Who misses out when you choose to doubt yourself rather than believe in the truth of your brilliant light? You've got everything you need right inside of you to be masterful at claiming a high level of self-worth.

Be willing to do the self-development work so that you have abundant resources to thrive in this area. The benefits are endless. Share your joyful powerful self.

EXERCISES

GET GUMPTION

Have lunch with yourself as if you are a big shot executive taking a lunch break. If you are at a restaurant, imagine you "own the place".

JOURNAL THIS:

- ◊ Why would I NOT to be brilliant and fabulous?
  List three reasons.
- ◊ Who am I depriving when I doubt myself?
  List three people or groups.

GET UNPLUGGED

When we value ourselves deeply, we create love and success wherever we go.

MEDITATE THIS:

- ◊ Breathe in the fragrance of a flower as if you are smelling it with your entire awareness. Let each breath replace any doubt or concern.
- ◊ Whisper your name to yourself with a tone of honor and loving respect. Whisper it over and over with each breath in and each breath out.

24

Are You Keeping Up With The Jonses?

Do you imagine "the better life" that appears to be happening right here in our community or even in your own neighborhood, without considering the drain on your energy and sense of joy?

The definition of "Keeping up with the Joneses" is the comparison to one's neighbor as a benchmark for social lifestyle or the accumulation of material goods.

Failure to "Keep up with the Joneses" is perceived as demonstrating socio-economic or cultural inferiority.

Ouch! That's a huge amount of pressure and expectation! The ironic part in this cycle of comparison, is that you never *ever* make it. There can never be an arrival at the destination of "I'm Beyond the Jonses" because "The Jonses" are really just an imagined representation of what you "SHOULD" be having or doing that is more or better than what you are currently having or doing.

What a perfect set-up for perpetual struggle! It fuels the sabotaging belief that we are somehow "not enough". (Wrong!) These annoying "Jonses" are simply robbing us of our inner sense of fulfillment, of knowing that we are already wealthy beyond measure everywhere it really matters.

Life is rich with opportunities to "Keep Up." Do you notice areas of your life where you need MORE, simply because someone or somewhere in your social circle it's coveted?

Maybe it's wardrobe, or entertainment choices, or status symbols such as cars or jewelry or home décor. Maybe it's a title or a level of achievement. Do you notice wanting to share or show off acquisitions of any kind with a slight "keeping up with the Joneses" flair behind it?

Are you motivated by what others have or do as an influence for your own choices? Yes and yes. . . and remember not to be judgmental or critical of yourself, but rather just NOTICE – so that you make room for new choices.

Here is a powerful perspective: Make your life about shining your light instead.

Stop editing your brilliance. It's time to shine so others will benefit from what you have to offer.

If you are not so busy "keeping up" what would you be doing instead? Think of the qualities you see in someone who is "keeping up". Probably competitive, small-minded, selfish, self-absorbed, struggling, depleted, never satisfied. . . And now think of the qualities you would see in someone who is "shining their own light". Probably confidence, abundance, passion, inspired, on fire. Do you see the distinction between positive and negative qualities?

Three ways to live fully expressed:

1. **Pick one area of your life where can allow your gifts to shine.** Where can you take the lid off of your talents and really make a difference. At work? On a specific project? In your relationship? With your family? Are you hiding your

humor or your compassion or your generosity anywhere or with anyone? Just close your eyes and let the answer come from within.

2. **Ask yourself if you are afraid of your power or hiding what you have to offer.** We all have experiences that remind us it's better to "play it small." Now it's time to heal these conflicts and be the best human we are capable of being. Get the support you need to handle this.

3. **Step over your fear of being SELFISH.** Notice if you hold a belief that standing out brings too much attention to yourself

Shift your perspective and start having conversations that support the success you want in your life. Start by seeing the "Joneses" differently. What if they were a group of people dedicated to your fullest expression? Imagine them carrying torches and colorful banners that say, "Go, YOU!"

Imagine these "Joneses" singing words that inspired you to shine your brightest everywhere you are.

What if the "Jonses" only celebrated when you were living fearlessly? Imagine them doing an uplifting circle dance. The rest of the time they are like an inflatable doll laying flat until you show them a burst of your positive energy.

NOW you can shine, and NOW you can be free of that tired old "Jonses" story.

When we shine our own light, our equality is illuminated and it's easier to see that we are all ONE.

EXERCISES

GET GUMPTION

Pick two ways to stand out this week and make them happen. You could add something different to your normal routine such as playing music, or being in silence instead... you could wear a new color or eat a new food.

JOURNAL THIS:

- ◊ Where is it easy for you to shine your light?
- ◊ Where do you dim your light?

GET UNPLUGGED

Just look around. See from the wisdom that nobody is higher or lower, no one is more superior or inferior than another. Everybody is unique without comparison.

MEDITATE THIS:

- ◊ I am fulfilling my own potential in the best way I know how. Imagine this happening.
- ◊ When I listen with my heart, I hear the songs of support. Listen into your primary relationship.

25

What Happens When You Are in a Slump?

It's inevitable that we get stuck at different times and in different areas of our lives. The good news is that we never have to stay stuck. What is a slump?

Being in a rut, or feeling like you're stuck. Maybe you are experiencing a mental funk, an emotional low, a physical drag, or an overall down and out.

Three strategies to get out of a slump.

First, think about your timing. Do you agree that timing is everything in most circumstances?

Honor your internal clock. If you are more creative mid-morning, do not schedule or plan on creative projects at the end of the day. If you are more flexible and motivated to work out at 8:30am rather than 7am, it would make sense to move your workout to a later time. Why is it that we force activities to happen at times when we know we will not get the best result?

If you are listening to your inner critic make excuses like, "but I have to stick to my schedule" or "I can only..." or "they won't let me..." you need to take charge immediately and make the change anyway.

Timing is huge influence and will make the difference between being stuck and being free. Our excuses or limitations are only in our own minds and until you find the courage to take action and make the change, you will stay in your slump.

Second, take an inventory. Do you know what you have, what you need, what you potentially will want to add? These are methods to understand progress. How can you move forward when you don't know where you've been, what you've already moved into and what's between where you are and where you are going?

The focus is to track your progress. When is the last time you acknowledged yourself for something measurable that you did?. When I ask my clients to do this, their responses feel remarkable every time because they "forget" to take stock and are not used to celebrating daily accomplishments. It's powerful to acknowledge yourself out loud. Keep a rating of your relationship satisfaction. Keep a list of income or prospective income. Make a journal for fitness tracking. What else do you need to keep track of?

Third, keep things fresh. We do this in our refrigerators, so why not in our goals, relationships or businesses? It's human nature to respond positively to what is NEW. It's our nature to become neutral or immune to something helpful to us if we don't keep it fresh and compelling.

What is starting to go stale? What do you know you will never eat? Do you keep things that you know you will not want? Useless every time. Throw it out, or handle it so that it's not keeping you stuck. Make room for the new!

People who enjoy successful relationships will tribute their happiness to keeping it fresh, mixing it up and taking time out for doing something different. That is your key to get unstuck in any other area of your life. Freshen it up.

26

Am I Creating Distraction or Direction?

The best way to move forward is to shift away from what feels old or limiting, and move toward what feels new and expansive. Ask questions. Get curious about your motivations. Check in with yourself, "Does this (thought or action) create distraction or does it create direction?"

Every thought or choice you make is toward direction OR toward distraction. There is only one choice. Nothing in the middle and no in-between. Here's the scoop on distraction: it keeps you stuck.

Distraction is a movement away from productivity or momentum and might temporarily be wonderful, but the cost of losing your focus and commitment to what moves you forward is often high.

Cultivate your ability to make this powerful choice. Be awake to this choice and make it consciously. Unplug from anything that distracts you. Unplugging is a conscious choice.

Start small and build your strength.

The habit of asking yourself powerful questions is a great tool for staying on track, "Does this give me a sense of who I AM?" or, "Does this give me a sense of who I am NOT?"

Your answers don't matter as much as the choice you make TO ASK. The important part is to line yourself up with what you want. Awareness is your treasure chest.

Feeling stuck, then getting unstuck, this is a cycle. Being distracted can also be a place where insights, healing and breakthroughs happen. We just don't want to STAY stuck, or BE distracted beyond what's needed. We want to be resilient and flexible. Not stagnant and stiff. Yes, there are gifts in every single experience. Be awake to your process in order to choose forward momentum.

"Do I feel resistance or do I feel peace?" Great question, because if your choice is not peace, then what is it? Do you want to choose again? The best way to move beyond anger toward another person is to say a prayer for them. When you choose peace instead of anger, only one thing can happen in your relationship with the other person: Your behavior will be different, or, you won't care anymore. Either way, you just bought yourself wonderful freedom!

Imagine your life as a platform. You can jump up from the platform, create from it and grow from it, always having the ability to expand it. What happens when you stay put? Don't use it? Ask yourself, "Am I stuck on my platform? Or, Am I using my platform to create/contribute/learn/connect?"

27

Are You Ready for a New Chapter?

Our lives have an unlimited amount of new chapters. Whenever we are willing to let something go, or to step in a new direction, a new chapter begins. Typical "new chapters" include major events such as weddings, graduations, funerals, moving, new careers, having children, etc.

There are also milestone events such as making a new connection, rearranging furniture, organizing something differently, starting a new project, reading a life-changing book, beginning a new routine (exercise, eating, spiritual practice, date night.)

Create more meaning in your life by paying attention to every single new chapter, whether it is big or small. Most of the time, a new chapter is a feeling or perception we create in our mind. The treasure is in feeling inspired and uplifted by crossing into "the new" and experiencing the joy of renewal, rejuvenation and growth.

If we are not growing, we are not LIVING. Why not accent the markers of growth and change by giving them positive meaning?

Examples of thoughts that create meaning:

"I am exactly where I'm supposed to be."

"I'm now ready for anything!"

"I learned so much, I can handle whatever is next."

"It's getting better and better all the time."

"This feels refreshed and open. I welcome the next level with eager anticipation."

ALL new chapters are an opportunity to assign meaning that feels empowering. Think of a new chapter as a moment in life to designate a powerful opening, as if you are setting up a permanent doorway into an arena of good that you can access over and over.

It's as if you are creating new ways to see yourself in the Light of growth, expansion and goodness. Every day is an opportunity to start a new chapter.

We know from experience how we FEEL about something stays with us longer than what we see or hear. Our heart holds more power than the experience we have in our head, especially when it comes to making an event mean something positive.

Notice how the difference between experiencing an event in a logical or rational way rather than feeling like it has special meaning is far more memorable and influential.

Mark a new chapter in your life by incorporating a ritual.

Think of ritual as a "symbolic behavior". It's taking the time to do something meaningful. It's taking a commemorative action in physical form. Rituals are a powerful way to get over the past, and move forward.

Eight common rituals:

- ◊ Burning letters or old pictures.
- ◊ Writing a letter to express feelings and never sending it.
- ◊ Going to a location where something "began" to contemplate or reflect.
- ◊ Lighting a candle with an intention.
- ◊ Putting certain flowers in the house.
- ◊ Burning sage to clear something away.
- ◊ Preparing a special dish for a loved one.
- ◊ Using a gratitude journal or jar.

Simple rituals help us find more "closure" with our experiences. This makes it easier to move on and embrace the future. It's powerful to close one door before opening another. Clean transitions are powerful.

It's important to know that there is no "right" or "wrong" way to do a ritual. The only thing that matters is *how they mean something* to the person doing the ritual.

I challenge you to play with more meaning in your life. What would you like to acknowledge about your current circumstances?

Can you create a simple ritual to mark the growth or change in your relationship? Think of this as the greatest gift you can give yourself.

You are taking the time to acknowledge where you have been and the person you were who did the best you could with everything you knew at the time, AND you are making it mean that you have grown and changed into an even greater person who is now doing something better and different!

28

Do You Think Too Much?

Get unstuck by relaxing your rational mind. We use it to make decisions and solve problems. This is the prefrontal cortex area of our brain, where we engage in critical thinking and self-monitoring.

Have you ever stopped and asked yourself, "What should I do or what should I think now?" Welcome to your rational or analytical mind. What if today, you put it down for a long nap?

Ask yourself:

"Am I feeling into this, or am I trying to figure it out?"

"Is my focus on thinking this through, or going with the flow?"

Asking the right question in your daily experiences will help you transform an unhealthy reliance on using only a small part of your brain. Just be open to the curiosity of HOW you are processing things and you can begin choose other options.

Be a gourmet chef with your own brain. The more choices you have, the tastier the dish!

Do you "think too much" and beat up your mind over continuously dwelling on questions you haven't answered? Letting go of your rational mind can bring relief and relaxation from accepting what you don't know. (sweet sigh of relief)

Notice of you are hesitating or doubting yourself. This is a great sign that you are "thinking too much" and it is blocking your creativity and spontaneity. Let yourself go!

Instead of thinking or worrying about what you are doing, just DO and BE with it instead. Imagine an activity where you lose track of time in a pleasurable or fulfilling way. That is an example of your ability to DO and BE with something rather than thinking about it too much.

Too much thinking is the main culprit for any kind of creativity. It also sabotages our talent for great conversation. If you ever struggle with social skills you are likely "thinking too much". Make room for your natural responses rather than rehearsing or editing everything you want to say. Ask yourself, "Am I feeling natural here, or am I feeling rehearsed?"

Looking for enlightenment? The primary instruction along that path is to release judgment. We must strive to be Non-judgmental beings in the world. "Thinking too much" causes us to form beliefs, categorize people and things, and become critical of ourselves and others.

Figure out how to let go and become less judgmental and kinder to yourself and others. (Hint: stop thinking too much.)

Do you realize how much energy you spend ruminating on specific things? How exhausting! Your poor brain can only process so much at once. Imagine the increase in mental resources coming into the present moment and paying full attention to what is in front of you.

Ask yourself, "Am I fully present right now?"

And, "What can I let go if in THIS moment?"

How are you doing with being 100% happy in your life? Check in with yourself about the need to justify everything you like. Do you catch yourself justifying what makes you happy? How much energy or time are you spending being analytical about why you like something?

Become adept at navigating your emotions. Use your rational mind to help guide your way through emotions, but never expect to completely understand your feelings by thinking about them. The main consideration is that your emotions and feelings are also a very important type of intelligence and understanding. Make room for the balance.

If you "think too much" you cannot fully understand yourself or the world around you. Release whatever fear or resistance you hold in order to stay in your limiting comfort zone of the analytical mind. It's beautiful out there!

Three questions to make room for "JUST BEING":

"Does this come from my heart, or does this come from my head?"

"Can I think less and feel more in THIS situation?"

"Is this an opportunity to "stop thinking too much?"

29

Are You Easily Offended?

Have you ever met "that person" who perceives everything as a personal attack?

Being offended is about feeling insulted, hurt, provoked or upset. The compelling perspective is that only YOU can create your experience. So, being offended is a choice. You are simply receiving a communication and you are choosing to make it mean something that "offends" you. Or, (even worse) you are choosing to use the communication to indulge in your own story.

Have you ever been offended without knowing the intention of the other person's communication? There is your problem. You are putting your ego and your self-absorbed needs in front of hearing or receiving a communication objectively, rather than the meaning you attach to it. Huge difference. Understand the value of the popular saying, "Get out of your own way." When you do, you are positioned to respond with a genuine and generous heart. Now you are making room for productive communication.

Here is a relevant quote from an unknown author: *"If one ventures a word with you, will you be offended? But who can keep from speaking?"*

When someone indulges their ego by getting offended – do you notice how the gift or the potential of the conversation is stopped? Suddenly there is no room for an open exchange. There is no room for collaboration.

The offended ego has taken the stage in a self-absorbed quest for fulfillment. Imagine having more room to dance in the flow of the music, across a huge open dance floor, rather than getting cut-in or cut-off by a needy ego.

When you feel offended ask yourself, "Where am I coming from right now?" Coach yourself to catch your own story. Look at "what do I need right now?" that you can responsibly give to yourself rather than manipulating others by getting offended or making it "all about you."

If you feel irritated or annoyed or angry, you are giving meaning to something in a way that perpetuates your own story about whether you are in abundance or whether you are in scarcity.

Notice if you are coming from LOVE or coming from FEAR and how your story is different from either mindset. Catch your story in a gentle way with yourself. You are always growing by having the choice to step into a new story.

Being easily offended can now be a self-coaching tool to step out of your limiting story if you have the gumption to do the work of noticing and catching yourself.

What can we do instead of being easily offended? Be comfortable listening to opposing information and opinions.

Check yourself with a scale of 1 – 10. One means you are easily offended and 10 means you are simply comfortable and curious. If you are below a 5, get some support to work toward a 10. If you are between 5 – 10, notice what you can do to get to a 10 and do it each day.

Demonstrate your commitment to being open and comfortable rather than offended.

So, what is best when something truly does offend you? Think of the information as "poorly delivered criticism" instead of "offensive insults". The best response isn't to get offended, it's to offer a helpful suggestion on how you'd like to receive feedback in the future. This way you take charge of your own experience and make it positive.

The booby prize for the poor ego that twists everything into a personal attack is that in the end they have compromised their best efforts. They lose out on every possibility. They sabotage themselves because others quickly grow tired of walking on eggshells around them and retreat or limit participating with them.

An easily offended person will somehow turn *anything* into an insult. Take time to notice what triggers your offended feelings. See if you can respond by embracing the opportunity to sharpen your thoughts and skills. Take on an empowering belief that "feeling offended gives me the opportunity to see disagreements as a way to improve my skills."

Your new positive belief gives you curiosity toward the communication rather than an ego-based reaction. Curiosity is much prettier than ego. You can ask for more details, ask to hear more examples, inquire about the meaning behind the statements. . . This approach yields a richer harvest of potential.

Getting offended is just a stop sign dripping with the sweat of self-absorption.

Hold the space for yourself and others this week to be grounded and self-confident no matter what anyone says.

30

Do You Need to Be Right?

Would you like to be free and peaceful more of the time? Add new dimension to your life by letting go of needing to be right.

To get the most out of this article, stop right now and notice what you think it means to be right. Make at note of it. Then compare your understanding at the end of this article to where you are right now.

Have fun "catching yourself in action" around how easy it is to think you know something (or think you are right about something) when really, your opportunity is to be open to something bigger instead.

My Life Coach, Debbie Leoni uses a story in her workshops. It illustrates our obsession with being right in a fun way. She asks her participants to "Pick up a pencil. Is it a pencil? How do you know it's a pencil? Do you think I am asking a silly question? Are you committed to it being a pencil? What if you were an Aborigine in Australia and you picked up a pencil. Then what would it be? Kindling for a fire? Something to hold long hair into a bun?"

Notice that when you let go of being right about what YOU think something is, you can be open to other information.

Being stuck in life happens when our ideas get small and our thinking stays small, which creates patterns causing a rut. The need to be right is a huge contribution to small thinking. It's interesting to get in touch with the part of ourselves wanting to be right, because the irony of feeling puffed up sitting higher is really just an illusion covering up a very small and ego-based position.

If you can release your attachment to being right about a conversation, or a position, or the meaning of something, you will become more interested in other people's point of view. What would be wonderful about being open to other people's opinions rather than stuck in your own stubborn or righteous stance?

Consider what you have to lose by "being right." Consider it as a game you play to WIN. And the more committed you are to winning, the more likely you will be right. When you land in the place of being the one who is right, check in. Are you alone? Or are you enjoying the gifts of union and collaboration and synergy? Maybe not a true "win" after all.

Needing to be right is a lonely experience. Tell yourself this truth and you will automatically release your resistance to being "wrong".

Look into all areas of your life. Pick the one where you are most struggling. Let's take finances for an example. Are you right about why you don't have enough? Are you right about your excuses? Do you want to be right, or do you want to fix it?

Let's look at relationships. Are you right about what is possible or not possible with the other person?

If you ARE right, then you have just limited yourself to one path. When you release the stubbornness or righteousness of hoarding all the "truth", then you can see an open landscape with unlimited paths.

Three questions to explore your need to be right:

"What am I afraid of being or seeing if I surrender being right?"

"What illusion do I buy into by being right?"

"What do I have to make wrong, in order to uphold my righteous position?"

Notice how you make another person wrong. (Judgment)

Do you make their experience or abilities wrong?

Better yet, if you are right, are you really just making someone else wrong?

There is unlimited exploration that will always lead to a treasure chest of positive things when it comes to releasing your need to be right.

Think of someone you know who always needs to be right. What qualities would you use to describe that person? Your list may include stubborn, selfish, rigid, strong willed, and powerful.

These qualities are not always negative. The point is to notice if they serve you or if they sabotage you.

Now assign qualities to someone you know who isn't caught up in needing to be right. Your list may include resilient, receptive, creative, open, giving, spontaneous, and powerful.

Did you notice I included "powerful" on both lists? Now you get to choose what expression of power is most attractive to you.

It's a perceived power to feel right. It's a powerful experience when you don't need to be right.

Choose. Let Go. Be happy.

SECTION FOUR:
Lift Your Point of View

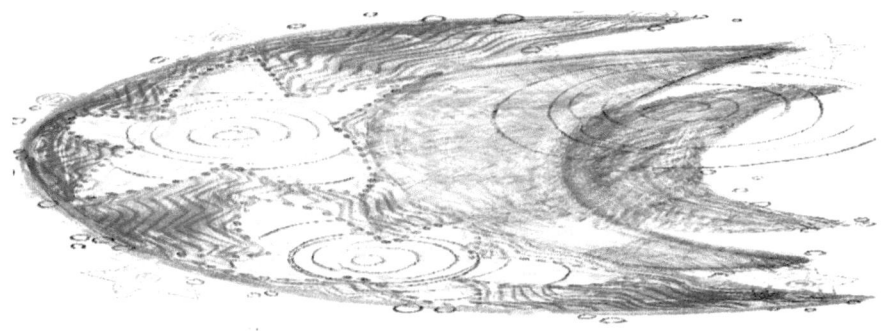

"Do not conform any longer to the pattern of this world, but be TRANSFORMED by the renewing of your mind."

Romans 12:2

THIS SECTION INCLUDES POINTS OF VIEW TO HELP YOU:

- ✓ Make wise choices, knowing you are worthy.
- ✓ Get out of your own way.
- ✓ Commit to a life of expression, growth and living fully.
- ✓ Acknowledge your triumphs and celebrate your milestones.
- ✓ Be happier by letting go of desires.
- ✓ Express PEACE through choices, actions and thoughts.
- ✓ Build trusting relationships with lasting value.
- ✓ Be free from disempowering thoughts.
- ✓ See the gift and perfection of everything in life.
- ✓ Say "Yes" or "No" with positive boundaries.

31

You Easily Distracted?

Do you struggle with overwhelm and distraction at times? Do you want to be focused and productive without falling off track so easily? Welcome to the distraction-rich environment of today's world!

Life will always pull your attention away or distract you. If you want to manage your distractions, learn what they are and where they originate. Then you can decide to stop and choose differently.

It's very helpful to notice the attention levels of children and how they deal with distractions. They are naturally resilient and much more present in the moment. Now you can look with compassion at your own resistance to distractions and see if you are making yourself wrong or beating yourself up when you lose focus.

What do you need to easily bounce back into your groove? (With the freedom of a child?)

Here is an empowering perspective: If there is always something to distract us, we simply are being called into the self-discipline it takes to hold our focus.

If you can exercise more gratitude around your distractions, you can start seeing them as a positive influence on strengthening your focus.

"Thank you, distractions!"

The bottom line is that we must exercise the self-responsibility to CHOOSE the task we want to focus on. We must CHOOSE that it is not an option to get distracted. We must flex the muscle of staying with it. Not deviating. Following it through no matter what. Does that feel impossible?

Becoming aware of resistance is the first step to change. Now you can address the fears that are underneath the resistance.

Could it be fearing that you are not enough? Jackpot. If something resonates, it's worth checking into.

Try these ideas on for size to learn more about your fears:

"I'm not enough so I need to be available for everything around me so I can feel full rather than empty."

"I'm not enough to know the right thing to focus on."

"I'm not enough so I need to always do more, be more, and pay attention to more. . ."

Now that you have been brave enough to land at the core, let's turn it around.

Step out of deficiency into SUFFICIENCY.

Know you are sufficient. You are enough.

Truth be told, you have everything you need at this moment.

Now you can allow the possibility that you have what it takes to choose one thing that deserves your focus. You can commit to it with 100% of your attention and to move it forward before you move to something else.

You will be demonstrating to yourself that you choose wisely, that you don't abandon yourself, that you are worthy of your own attention, and that it matters.

Pretty soon your operative belief is that you choose wisely, you are there for yourself, you are worthy and you matter. You are living fully expressed.

EXERCISES

GOT GUMPTION

Eliminate your focus on "not enough." Make a list of 5 positive statements you will make when you catch yourself in a negative thought pattern. My favorite one is, "I Got This!"

JOURNAL THIS:

- ◊ What steps can you take to follow things through no matter what?
- ◊ What is in the way of your focus?

GET UNPLUGGED

You have your own brilliance. It shines through whenever you have great passion and interest. You must believe in your mind's ability to be brilliant.

MEDITATE THIS:

- ◊ I give my mind freedom for expression. Imagine this. Feel this way of being.
- ◊ My mind is like a crystal, naturally brilliant. Use a crystal or brilliant stone to focus on when you empty your mind by breathing slowly for several minutes.

32

How Do We Discover Our Limiting Beliefs?

Do you ever notice someone stumbling on the very edge of success and think "if they would just get out of their own way" the triumph would happen? Welcome to the presence of Limiting Beliefs.

Needing to "get over ourselves" or get out of our own way are both indications of limiting beliefs.

Our beliefs are simply statements that we tell ourselves that we have decided are true. A belief that is limiting would be a statement that keeps us small, or suppressed, or narrow-focused or stuck. A belief that only allows us one way to see something can turn out to be quite limiting.

HOW do we discover our limiting beliefs?

Six Symptoms of Limiting Beliefs:

1. You feel like you are pushing to make something happen. You might be forcing or directing something, and it feels like work. Your limiting beliefs are causing that experience.
2. You cannot let go or relax. You feel anxious or restless. Those are big red flags that your limiting beliefs are up for you to notice.
3. You react abruptly to other people. You "flip out" for no

apparent reason. You snap easily. There is a limiting thought pattern that causes all of those behaviors. You are not at peace, you cannot accept the situation as it is, and you are not welcoming the present moment.
4. You know something is NOT going to work. Make a list of all the reasons why something will not work and you will see plenty of limiting thoughts, choices or perspectives right there.
5. Procrastination. Yes, this just hides the deeper symptom that you are stuck. Being stuck is the direct result of a limiting belief.
6. Your results haven't changed. This is a guarantee that limited beliefs are present. Your internal world hasn't changed, so therefore your outer results stay the same.

Limiting beliefs keep you stuck, stagnant and without growth.

Putting awareness on these six symptoms of limiting beliefs is the key to unlocking the freedom and happiness that is possible for us every day of our lives. Awareness brings choice. When we choose to replace a limiting belief with a new belief about possibility or acceptance or self-love, we are moving forward and enjoying an enlivened life with great purpose.

The important conversation is about HOW we release our limiting beliefs.

Here are six methods for letting go:

Meditation

NLP (Neuro Linguistic Programing)

Prayer

Coaching Session

Yoga

Connecting with an insightful friend.

Letting go of just one limiting belief can create an impactful transformation in how you feel about yourself.

Being able to accept and welcome the present moment is the main practice for transforming limiting beliefs. The present moment is where we have the most choices and the most power. Unplug.

EXERCISES

GET GUMPTION

Make two columns on a poster board or flip chart and list out "OLD BELIEFS on one side and "NEW BELIEFS" on the other. Get used to replacing a limiting belief with a new, positive belief that supports your growth and creativity.

JOURNAL THIS:

- ◊ What is my "Big Belief" that keeps me stuck in the past?
- ◊ What beliefs from my fears?
  What would I believe if I was coming from love instead?

GET UNPLUGGED

Life is about liberating your potentials. To recognize oppression is to understand the freedom of yourself. You cannot know freedom without knowing oppression. See yourself in a new light, free from oppressive beliefs or choices, and you will fly!

MEDITATE THIS:

- ◊ My spirit is limitless and free.
- ◊ I sense the radiance of my spirit and I soar!

33

When is Criticism Your Best Friend?

It's certain in life that you will encounter criticism. Are you able to be "informed" by the criticism or do you get "activated" by the criticism? The trouble starts when the criticism bruises our ego or triggers an emotional response full of angst and fear.

The only way to avoid criticism is to say nothing, do nothing, offer nothing, and create nothing. Therefore, if you are not facing any critics, you are going the wrong way in life.

Start welcoming criticism as indicators that you are right on and doing great!

All you need is a thick skin, right? All you need is a strong filter to immediately categorize criticism into the "doesn't bother me" section of your life. Your goal would be to take the friction of criticism and use it to polish your brightly shining light.

Criticism comes in many forms. Beside the direct statements that are written or communicated openly, there are subtle cues we take from others that indicate a focus on our flaws or shortcomings.

Take any form of criticism that comes to mind and ask yourself, "What do I make it mean?" Notice what you assign to the critic or the criticizing comment. Are you perpetuating a negative reaction in yourself by assuming the worst? If you look at it from the opposite angle, can you find an opening to be neutral about the criticism and even welcome it as an opportunity to adjust yourself in a positive way?

What would it take to get to a place of complete gratitude for criticism you receive?

If your mindset allows a freedom to explore what matters to you and what doesn't, you can find gratitude for this useful information.

You must also have access to compassion for the critic. It's often true that the critical information is about the shortcomings or unhealed places in the critic themselves. Consider the source, the agenda (theirs not yours) and that if it's not face-to-face there are other complicating factors. Humans tend to treat others differently online than we do in person.

Online interactions distort reality and remove the power of empathy between people. Hiding behind a screen makes people feel anonymous and less likely to own their actions. If you keep these factors in mind, you will have a much easier time being resilient to negative effects of criticism.

Do what it takes to see the critic without any emotional connection. Imagine there is no other agenda than to be of service to you. This way you can respond with clarity rather than react with vulnerability. You can be in charge of what you make the information mean. It also allows you the ability to discard anything you don't want or need and continue moving forward unscathed. Take it in, see what serves, and easily trash (or recycle) the rest. Done deal, moving on.

It's reasonable to get tangled in the drama of negative emotions, especially when we are sensitive to the people around us or to the nature of what is being criticized. Since we are committed to a life of expression and growth and living as fully as possible, we must understand criticism if we want to sleep soundly at night.

We must recognize that great works are going to have critics. It's a given.

Some people have a natural disposition to focus on flaws. Accept that and stop making it mean that they are opposing "YOU". Some people are harsh by nature or have a disposition to "hater" rather than a "liker".

In a study published in the Journal of Personality and Social Psychology researches looked at the attitude of people who have a predisposition to focus on flaws alone. They end up hating or liking things for absolutely no reason. This is clear evidence that no matter what you do, a small group of people will oppose it, negate it, or criticism it without any reason. Sometimes it just takes extra effort to deal with this.

Why do we dwell on the negative criticism? Clifford Nass, a professor at Stanford University writes that "negative emotions generally involve more thinking, and the information is processed more thoroughly than positive ones. Thus, we tend to ruminate more about unpleasant events — and use stronger words to describe them — than happy ones."

To understand this is to give yourself a break and let the criticism flow through your experience easily and effortlessly rather than letting it derail you completely. What if you could experience zero recovery time from a critical input? There's a sweet goal.

Being criticized is going to happen. Take on the confidence needed to understand when to listen to a *real* critique. It's easy for others to be a critic. They are not risking anything, they are not facing any backlash. It takes guts to put yourself out there, to express yourself authentically. Go for it.

EXERCISES

GET GUMPTION

Anytime you find yourself in the tangle of criticism, get unstuck by talking it through with a trusted friend, mentor, coach, or work it through yourself by journaling or meditation. Schedule a meaningful conversation this week.

JOURNAL THIS:

- ◊ If you knew you couldn't fail, what would you do?
- ◊ Describe your inner voice that is critical. When do you hear it?

GET UNPLUGGED

Practice your inner-child's playfulness. Play at life. Learn how to practice whatever you want to do by playing at it. Take the pressure off yourself. Enjoy the journey of life because the journey IS life.

MEDITATE THIS:

- ◊ I love myself for taking the risk of living out loud.
- ◊ My creative self is fearless and bold.

34

Do You Make Your Milestones Empowering?

Our lives have an unlimited amount of new chapters. Whenever we are willing to let something go, or to step in a new direction, a new chapter begins. Typical "new chapters" include major events such as weddings, graduations, funerals, moving, new careers, having children, etc.

There are also milestone events such as making a new connection, rearranging furniture, organizing something differently, starting a new project, reading a life-changing book, beginning a new routine (exercise, eating, spiritual practice, date night.)

Create more meaning in your life by paying attention to every single new chapter, whether it is big or small. Most of the time, a new chapter is a feeling or perception we create in our mind. The treasure is in feeling inspired and uplifted by crossing into "the new" and experiencing the joy of renewal, rejuvenation and growth.

If we are not growing, we are not LIVING. Why not accent the markers of growth and change by making them mean something wonderful!?

Examples of thoughts that create meaning:

"I am exactly where I'm supposed to be."
"I'm now ready for anything!"
"I learned so much, I can handle whatever is next."
"It's getting better and better all the time."
"This feels refreshed and open. I welcome the next level with eager anticipation."

ALL new chapters are an opportunity to assign meaning that feels empowering. Think of a new chapter as a moment in life to designate a powerful opening, as if you are setting up a permanent doorway into an arena of good that you can access over and over. It's as if you are creating new ways to see yourself in the Light of growth, expansion and goodness.

Every day is an opportunity to start a new chapter.

We know from experience how we FEEL about something stays with us longer than what we see or hear. Our heart holds more power than the experience we have in our head, especially when it comes to making an event mean something positive.

Notice how the difference between experiencing an event in a logical or rational way rather than feeling like it has special meaning is far more memorable and influential.

Use the power of ritual to make a new chapter more meaningful.

A ritual is a "symbolic behavior". It's about taking the time to do something meaningful. Ritual is a commemorative action in physical form. Rituals are a powerful way to get over the past, and move forward.

Eight ideas for rituals:

1. Burning letters or old pictures.
2. Writing a letter to express feelings and never sending it.
3. Going to a location where something "began" to contemplate or reflect.
4. Lighting a candle with an intention.
5. Putting certain flowers in the house.
6. Burning sage to clear something away.
7. Preparing a special dish for a loved one.
8. Using a gratitude journal or jar.

Simple rituals help us find more "closure" with our experiences. This makes it easier to move on and embrace the future. It's powerful to close one door before opening another. Clean transitions are powerful. It's important to know that there is no "right" or "wrong" way to do a ritual.

I challenge you to play with more meaning in your life this week. What would you like to acknowledge about your current circumstances?

Can you create a simple ritual to mark the growth or change in your relationship? Think of this as the greatest gift you can give yourself. You are taking the time to acknowledge where you have been and the person you were who did the best you could with everything you knew at the time, AND you are making it mean that you have grown and changed into an even greater person who is now doing something new and improved!

35

Are You Willing to Simplify Your Desires?

What if you could focus more on the pleasure of life by giving up just one of your desires?

It's time to de-clutter your desires. Our desires can be endless. There is no shortage of money, technology, stereo systems, furniture, clothes, shoes, food, sleep, cocktails, toys and whatever else we want. How many of these things do you think you need?

If we continually go after all of these "things" that society tells us will make our life happier or better, we are missing the chance to make a smarter choice about our personal fulfillment.

Let's keep it simple by just eliminating one desire at a time. After all, the more you desire, the more work you will have to do to get it. Yes, if you really want something, it's a positive choice to strive for it. You must first be clear that you are making the choice to put the energy into work and striving.

A study showed that by temporarily giving up a desire for a period of time, the pleasure received from getting the desire was actually improved! An experiment was done where participants abstained from eating chocolate for one week. They reported greater happiness the next time they ate chocolate compared to the participants who could eat as much chocolate as they wanted.

What are you letting yourself do or have too much? Where can you make a conscious choice to improve your satisfaction?

Based on this experiment, what is possible for your own happiness if you try living with one less desire for even one day? I challenge you to do this for a week.

Consider that life really can be happier when you find joy in the simple pleasures. "Take time to stop and smell the roses" is perfect wisdom here. It's true that we don't have to "DO" extravagant things to find joy when we can watch a sunset, or play with a pet, or appreciate a flower instead. You can stop feeling the need to fulfill desires simply by finding that happiness in every day occurrences.

Gratitude comes to mind. When we are thankful or in a grateful state of mind, it is naturally easier to find simple pleasures (and feel happier). Revive your gratitude practice. Start a gratitude journal.

Transformation is exciting when you can uncover an old belief that isn't serving you. Then replace it with a NEW belief that moves you forward.

A limiting belief about happiness is this: "Having the things I want makes me happy."

A new positive belief about happiness is this: "Becoming happier is about letting go of certain desires, rather than fulfilling them."

Can you sense the freedom and simplicity of happiness that starts opening up for your life?

Let's pursue being happy with less. If that is too much to take on, how about exploring the benefits of living with less? Look for the key areas in your life where you can make an impact.

Find ways to ask for "less" and instead make room in your own heart or "more".

36

Want More PEACE in Your Life?

It's not uncommon to desire peace in daily life. We want to feel the joy of balance or stillness or room to breathe as we take on the fullness of our lives. Almost every single client I have worked with over the years strives for a more peaceful way of living, or more presence of peace in their life.

If you had more peace in your life, what would be happening? What would you feel that you're not feeling now? What would the presence of PEACE in your life mean for your family or friends or loved ones?

Begin your quest for peace by getting in touch with WHY you want it. Knowing your "why" gives you access to your core beliefs. Why do you believe that a more peaceful life is better? When you express your beliefs about peace, it's easy and natural for others to support you and get involved with your efforts because they feel aligned with your foundation. We never have to make change happen alone. We are always one moment away from great support, and all we have to do is be open and allow the connection.

A powerful way to create peace in life is to hold the intention to express peace in every action or choice you make in a given day or situation you encounter. This is a natural catalyst to the flow of peace in and out of your life. Activate peace anywhere and any way you can, and you are activating the part of yourself that IS Peace. A much easier approach than managing it or taking on a list of tasks to promote peace for yourself.

Nine ways to add more PEACE to your life.

Rate yourself for each of the following experiences using a scale of 1 – 10.

"1" being non-existent, "10" being totally happening.

1. My ability to enjoy each moment. _____
2. Letting it happen rather than making it happen._____
3. My ability to love without expecting anything._____
4. Having occurrences of smiling in a day. _____
5. Having episodes of appreciation in a day._____
6. Never interpreting the actions of others._____
7. Losing interest in judging others or myself. _____
8. Feeling connected with others and nature. _____
9. Eliminating my choice to worry._____

Challenge yourself to take your ratings to a higher level. This list will be your "Criteria for Peace". These are nine essential things you need to master in order to have more peace in your life.

Make note of what you need to change or shift in order to move from a five or six all the way up to a ten. Ask yourself, "What is in the way of being at a ten in all of my ratings?" Schedule a session with me to explore your options and make a plan to start getting results right away. How badly do you really want more peace? Enough to step out of your comfort zone? Enough to make a commitment to daily actions and be held accountable?

Adding peace to your life can be a slow and simple process. Consider taking one small step at a time. The rewards are huge!

37

Do You Embrace the Power of Trust?

Our lives are filled with areas to build or create trust. Think of trust as the foundation for all relationships. Without trust there is nothing to build on. We have endless opportunities to trust everywhere we turn in life. Trusting a partner, trusting ourselves, trusting in a positive outcome, trusting a friend, trusting that a commitment is honored. We also get to practice building trust everywhere we turn.

On a business or career level, notice the profound role trust plays in your work. It's a common fact that we are all selling something whether we are directly involved in a sales capacity or not. We want to persuade others to do something, or help others find a better solution, or influence an outcome in some way. To see these things as "selling" helps you value building trust in order to have successful relationships.

Building trust means allowing it to thrive and grow. We need to build trust in areas where trust is broken or needs to be repaired.

We are humans who make mistakes and if trust is effected, we get the opportunity to earn trust again. (and again, and again. . .)

The process of building trust is perpetual. Imagine it never ending, only expanding and strengthening and always giving back. Building trust creates gifts.

What if your priority is to always build trust? If trust is a bank account in your relationships, are you depositing trust every chance you can? When your relationships have a healthy bank account, it's easy to draw out what you need whenever you need it while maintaining a wealthy balance. There's a winning priority!

How do you build trust in any relationship? It starts with communication. **I'll give you the bottom line first: You must get the other person talking about themselves and then, you must stop and listen.** Truly listen with all your might. Unless you are an exception, you are probably ripe for improvement in this area. So take it on without resistance and position yourself for the benefit of enjoying deeper trust. Because where there is trust, there is everything.

Instructions for communication that builds trust:

Never apply the conversation to yourself.

In my many years of facilitation and coaching groups I see people miss opportunities by making conversations all about themselves. Often times they don't even recognize what they are doing, although it's obvious to the recipient who the conversation is about and then trust and connection go right out the window.

You must ALWAYS redirect the conversation BACK to their original point, and then move it forward by either asking a correlated question or by making a validation of their point in a way that expands it or advances it. The idea is to STAY with their track on the topic. Never jump the track until theirs is 100% complete. The moment you can acknowledge a completion of THEIR track, you have created powerful connection of trust. Acknowledge their track with statements like, "I see it your way now (and reflect it back)" Or, "Let me get the clear picture on your point, it's (and reflect it back)." Or, you can reflect it back to them in your own words and then ask, "Is that accurate?"

It takes great effort and focus to hold a conversation toward the other person. Our natural tendency is to jump tracks, especially when we are emotionally involved because we think it's our job to "convince or lead or guide" the person forward. You must surrender these tendencies and trust in the power of listening instead. When this is done successfully, you will gather positive evidence that this way of relating is very powerful and with consistency and practice it will become second nature.

And. . . it's much more fun!

Here is the best way to achieve trust-building communication: Limit yourself to 60-second answers, maximum, then turn it back to the other person. Anything more is about you, not about them. And it's about them. Always.

I challenge you to use a timer with someone that is comfortable to practice with. You may be surprised to discover the discrepancy between your answers and their answers. Who holds the most "conversational real estate" in the relationship? What if you made it equal? Better yet, what if you made sure their real estate was always growing and expanding?

The powerful benefit to this is the experience of being valued, being seen and heard, being honored and being supported. When these feelings are generated through trust building communication, you are creating a powerful connection that literally will get you everything you want and more. Somehow we have missed the teachings to strengthen these skills. Tomorrow is a new day. Implement and bask in the wonderful results!

38

How is Your Self Esteem?

Are your riding high with banners of love and joy flowing in the breeze? Are you pretending it's sunny when there's a storm brewing inside? Are you wobbling and spinning wondering what's wrong or missing? Self-esteem is what you think, believe and feel about yourself. It's not something we have or don't have, it's something that is thriving and healthy, or depleted and struggling.

When our self-esteem is healthy, we make choices that match up with our peace of mind, values and our dreams.

Imagine your self-esteem is a scale of 1-10. Ten is healthy/thriving and one is depleted/struggling. Where are you? What is in between where you are and ten? It will be an ongoing process to move up the scale. It is achieved through regular strengthening and maintaining, just like working a muscle.

A "Self-Esteem Checkup" is extremely important because nothing sticks if your self-esteem is low. Without self-esteem, you have nothing to build on. It's like being a fly-strip with no glue. There you are flowing in the breeze thinking you are on purpose, trying to make a useful contribution and you never feel good about getting results or fulfillment.

Things are obviously not happening in your favor through no fault of your own except that your self-esteem (YOUR GLUE!) is missing. You've got to address the issue at the GLUE level. Not the surface level of "am I doing it right?" In this creative "fly strip analogy" would it be productive to question the way you flow, or which way you face or the location you are in, rather than looking deeper to see if your GLUE is fresh and present and intact? Obviously not. If your GLUE is strong/healthy, you will attract more flies than you could handle. (And as a fly strip, this is a GOOD thing.)

This is similar to filling a gas tank with a hole in it. Look at the types of questions that would come up if you are driving around in life with a leaking tank: "Why am I always out of gas?" "I need gas again???" "I feel like every time I start to get going I have to stop." "I never have enough." "This is costing me too much." "I'm doing this wrong, or, I'm not good enough to do this well!"

I see the drag-down factor of this kind of thinking everywhere in life. We try over and over to fix it with several different approaches, but we must stop to look deeper instead.

Your Self-Esteem Checkup Starts Here:

Notice your feelings, and look at what thoughts you are having that cause these feelings.

- ◊ Does this thought increase my self-esteem?
- ◊ Am I empowered or disempowered by this thought?

NOW you can choose new thoughts instead. Choose these types of thoughts to support healthy self-esteem:

- ◊ I choose the thoughts I think.
- ◊ I love thinking confident thoughts.
- ◊ I am the one telling the story, and I make it a good one.
- ◊ I have all the support and resources I need.

The very act of noticing your thoughts is truly empowering. You are sending a strong message to your brain that says, "I am totally in charge of my thoughts." This demonstration takes you WAY farther down the path toward a "ten."

One winning strategy for increasing your self-esteem:

Congratulate yourself every time you have an empowered thought. You have made the choice. Acknowledging yourself for a positive thought goes a long way to reinforce your healthy self-esteem strength.

When you have a disempowered thought, stop and acknowledge yourself as well! Give recognition to yourself for NOTICING the thought. Take a deep breath and see how responsible you are being for your life, fore choosing to love and accept yourself. Celebrate that you are IN the process of transformation. So many people miss this step. It's very powerful.

You are on your way with a full tank, intact with powerful fuel in abundance, and you have all the "glue" you need to perform at your greatest potential.

39

What is Perfect About THIS Moment?

Perfection is overrated, but seeing how the MOMENT is perfect, well, that's genius.

I have the reputation for nudging people into "seeing what's perfect" no matter what is going on.

Imagine the last time you felt challenged or stuck or in the midst of deep emotions. Feel it? Now consider my next question: "What is totally perfect about what's happening here?"

Whoosh. You either land in resistance, or you begin to shift. There are gifts in both landing spaces, and good coaching is about not making your reactions WRONG. . . because both will set you free (eventually). Now you can look for the perspective you want to choose.

If you first land in resistance, such as shouting with indolence, "WHAT?? Right now is PERFECT??" Or if you immediately doubt or feel annoyed by such a silly or useless perspective, then own your glorious resistance and start from there. The gift of your resistance is that it launches you into problem-solving mode. Since you were dismissing what's happening, you are likely wanting to do whatever it takes to resolve it and move on. The opposition you are feeling can be a great catalyst for change or improvement. OR, it can keep you stuck. Your choice.

If you first land in an open position to shift, you are already activating a positive mindset of eager anticipation.

Six qualities are activated in this positive mindset: Gratitude, receptivity, resilience, willingness to be vulnerable, letting go, creative thinking.

Does it start to feel easier and smoother by reading all of those attractive words?

The big deal about taking a position to shift is that you are activating GRATITUDE.

When you look for the perfection in what's currently happening, you are automatically moving into the energy of Gratitude, which is a powerful way to live. Author Neale Donald Walsch expresses the power of gratitude this way, "Saying thanks for something before you get it is a declaration of absolute clarity that you are going to receive it. This shift of energy is neither pointless nor meaningless." Take that to your journal!

An easy access point to seeing the perfection, even when your situation seems unbearable, is to look for what you can appreciate about it. Sometimes it's difficult to do this on our own. Ask someone who has earned the right to share your emotions with you for help. Find a mentor or coach or counselor to talk through your issue and support you in seeing ways that you can understand the perfection of it. See the value in making this shift, and the support you need will become available for you.

Start by feeling into your challenge, and looking for one thing you can be thankful for about it.

Simply asking to see what MIGHT be perfect about your situation opens the door toward acceptance, which moves you forward.

Next, start looking at HOW it's serving you. Really be honest and see what you are getting out of the whole thing. Because it would not be happening if it wasn't serving you in some way. That's just how life works.

Finally when you begin to get a perspective on how it's benefitting you, it's time to embrace that it's perfect in that way.

Keep in mind, this is great work! And now I challenge you to make it easy and fun!

How would your life be different at a higher level of mastery in your self-awareness?

Five ways to claim a new perspective:
- Talk about it.
- Write about it.
- Cook a meal for it.
- Share it.
- Sing about it.

Can you do something that demonstrates the love for yourself that you discovered through being curious? I bought myself a new coffee mug and I consciously use it only when I'm celebrating a breakthrough.

And I like to use it often!

40

Should I Get Involved?

Consider some accurate statements with me: Happy people have good support networks. People that are involved in groups, causes and other community projects tend to be happier and more satisfied with their lives.

Groups that are focused on service or philanthropy or non-profit contributions give people a great sense of purpose and contribution that results in a happier and more fulfilling life. Take a personal consideration, "what are you involved in?"

Where are you over-involved or where do you want to be more involved? Where do you resist and where do you embrace when it comes to your involvement?

How does "BEING INVOLVED" influence your life? Notice any resistance that comes up when you have a request or opportunity to get involved. Notice if you are always yearning to get involved, or that you wish you could be more involved. It's natural to be initially contrary or initially accepting.

This can simply be your nature to respond either way, and then you can think it through or explore it further to see if it makes sense for you. Learn enough to see if you feel excited about it.

Do you have opportunities in your life where people are asking you to "get involved?" There is a large spectrum that goes from "there is too much for me to do" to "I wish I had more to do" when it comes to involvement.

When life gets busy and full, the areas that get eliminated first are often volunteering or involvement in an organization that you simply do not have time for any more. Taking steps on either side of this conversation can bring immediate feelings of accomplishment.

This topic brings out one of the top issues in personal satisfaction, which is being able to say "NO". Being able to say "YES" to the things that help us grow and evolve creates fulfillment.

What if you could embrace a new opportunity without any fear? What if you could take on a new project or contribute to a group with ease and confidence? (no guilt or negative self-talk!).

And, equally as important, what if you could clearly see what you need to clear away in your life in order to enjoy more balance and be fully present to the priorities that are in place currently?

Make this happen for yourself by taking the time to tap your inner clarity. You already know these types of answers. Just give yourself room to think it through and simply allow it.

If that sounds vague and cheesy to you, I challenge you to see it as a purposeful action step and then actually do it without judging yourself. The action of getting quiet and looking inside will always yield productive results.

The action of expanding your thinking or expanding your perception will always make room for you to see something differently, which is a huge contribution to your ability to ALLOW what really matters to come through. This is a proven method that always produces successful results. Go be cheesy. As a matter of fact, be VERY extremely cheesy. You will learn to love the powerful results.

When older people look back on their lives with good feelings, it's usually about things they said yes to, and areas where they became involved. Involvement in groups and projects brings measurable satisfaction and accomplishment to life. The people we meet, the relationships we form and the experiences we have are all priceless and held closest to our heart as time goes by.

SECTION FIVE:
Visualize the Bigger Picture

"With the new day ahead comes new strength and new thoughts."

-Eleanor Roosevelt

THIS SECTION INCLUDES POINTS OF VIEW TO HELP YOU:

- ✓ Reframe negative qualities into inspiring positive qualities.
- ✓ Find balance as a process in your life, not a destination.
- ✓ Cultivate courage and fearlessly face the unknown.
- ✓ Manifest your dreams and idea with discipline.
- ✓ Enrich your life by expressing your genuine feelings.
- ✓ Own the power you have to inspire others.
- ✓ Give and receive reminders of your true self.
- ✓ Let go of attachments and beliefs that don't serve you.
- ✓ Celebrate each time you arrive "home" to your sweet self.
- ✓ Direct your energy and attention with positive results.

41

Can You "Find the Good" in Any Situation?

Finding a positive aspect in any situation is a worthy skill that will cultivate happiness and success in your life. Rate your ability to think positive on a scale of one to ten. Ten being masterful at turning any perspective or experience easily into something more positive. One being perpetual negativity, victimhood and no positivity in sight. If you are less than a ten, just notice what is in between where you are and where you would like to be.

Even though "finding the good" sounds simple, it can be a challenge to practice it, and sometimes can feel difficult to do. Face the challenge to "find the good" and make a powerful contribution to being happy.

Let's activate our positive mindset first. Mike Dooley says, *"The more you find good in another, the more you will find good in yourself."*

Success author Seth Godin writes, *"Instead of wondering when your next vacation is, maybe you should set up a life you don't want to escape from."* Powerful!

The best place to start any transformation is within yourself. Look at qualities in yourself and notice if you "find the good" in them, or if you judge them in a negative way.

Imagine the freedom and energy you have when you choose the positive perspective! You no longer have to compensate or tell yourself a story that supports the negative view. Now it's easy to see that when you "find the good" in your own self-expression, everything else opens toward the positive.

Have you ever been labeled defiant or demanding? What if instead you were being courageous and assertive? Notice where you shrink behind negative descriptions of yourself. Notice that when you "find the good" instead, you give yourself room to shine.

Instead of "bossy" you are a natural leader or an effective director. Instead of "conceited" you are valuing yourself and being confident.

What qualities stand out to you?

Affectionate (not clingy), Efficient (not compulsive), Easy-going (not dawdles), and Connected (not dependent). Do you see a pattern where you can go the extra mile to find the gift in any quality in order to turn it around to its positive side?

Sometimes when I am crabby, I prefer to think that I am communicating my needs.

Sometimes when I am dramatic, I prefer to think that I am emotionally aware and expressive. Sometimes when I am messy, I prefer to think I am open minded and easy going.

Maybe you see opportunities to "find the good" with your children? Or spouse, co-workers or family members? Anyone close to us will benefit in huge ways when we react to the positive side of their expressions rather than the negative. This choice is a natural way to shift any negative pattern. Try it!

Twelve qualities where you can "find the good":

Fearful becomes thoughtful and careful.

Foolish becomes fun loving.

Fussy becomes a strong sense of self.

Goofy becomes entertaining.

Impulsive becomes spontaneous.

Mean becomes power-seeking.

Naughty becomes an exploration of boundaries.

Nosey becomes a curiosity.

Shy becomes introspective.

Rigid becomes being organized.

Wanting attention becomes getting needs met.

Stubborn people are simply determined and persistent.

"Finding the good" is a powerful gift. When we choose to connect with the positive twist on things, we demonstrate to ourselves and others what matters. The positive energy can grow and effect everything. **Finding the good is a great way to ignite the flame of happiness everywhere.**

Aren't you tired of your old stories that are negative or self-depreciating? Start "finding the good" and watch your world shift immediately.

EXERCISES

GET GUMPTION

Pick one negative quality within yourself. This is a quality you are not proud of. Pretend you are wearing a T-shirt with this quality printed in big bold letters. How would you explain the gift of this quality to people who see you?

JOURNAL THIS:

- ◊ What qualities feed your flame? What qualities diminish your flame?
- ◊ What negative qualities do you need to let go of?

GET UNPLUGGED

Life is beautiful with a little madness in it. A little foolishness contributes humor and humbleness. A wise person is also a fool! Where can you make room for "keeping things weird"?

MEDITATE THIS:

- ◊ I am willing to see the greater version of every quality I express.
- ◊ No matter what is going on around me, I can go inside and find the good.

42

Is a Balanced Life REALLY Possible?

What if the idea of "Life Balance" is unattainable? Consider the notion that struggling to find balance in our lives only creates more of the stress and unrest that we are trying to overcome by searching for balance.

Laundry is part of life, and laundry is never done. We never say, "If only I had Laundry Balance!" We simply DO our laundry, and it is a cycle in our lives. Sometimes it piles up and sometimes is neatly organized and complete. For the moment. Because it is always happening. Maybe balance is really about being present with the cycles of our life.

Since life is always happening, never "done" and forever changing, why the obsessive desire for BALANCE?? Do you make yourself wrong when your laundry is piled up? And do you make yourself a superhero when your laundry is perfectly folded? Defining yourself by external circumstances doesn't serve you. Defining yourself by your internal state of well-being and your ability to CHOOSE well-being is much more self-loving. After all, it's JUST the laundry.

So how about, "It's JUST Life." Which is a great reminder to lighten up a little.

Let your life be messy. Sometimes. Remember that change is the only constant in your life, just like piles of clothes change from clean to dirty, and back to clean again. . . .

Laundry as a symbolic reference to most things in our life, is an ongoing cycle and we can choose to stop judging it or making parts of it wrong or negative. Where in your life can you say, "No big deal" and diffuse some of your controlling need to BALANCE?

I'm suggesting that letting go of the idea that a life in balance is somehow more fulfilling or more pleasing or more impressive is a smart move. Consider that when you believe you need more balance, you are actually sabotaging your peace of mind by indicating to yourself that your life is NOT fulfilled enough, NOT pleasing enough or NOT impressive enough.

That nasty "not enough" belief is the biggest culprit of all time! It robs our well-being and joy every time it shows up.

The golden ticket is inside the chocolate bar that says, "Embrace LIFE".

Life is ebb and flow. Life is messy and clean and messy again. Life is full of endless stops and starts. What does it mean to you to Embrace Life? Allow more ease? Give yourself permission to be ENOUGH no matter what is happening or not happening? Maybe there is something you could let go of in your life in order to feel more allowing of the process.

Think of balance as a process in your life, not a destination.

Balance is not a state that you earn or deserve by working hard to achieve it, because balance is totally subjective.

One person's life could look balanced to you, and another's life could look the opposite of balanced, and each person may report either balance or mayhem, depending on the meaning they attach to everything.

Notice where you can start attaching meaning to your life that reminds you of peace. Fulfillment. Well-being. Return to the Laundry analogy. What if you found balance every time you placed a load in the washer? Every time you put away folded clothes? Every time you felt grateful for clean clothes?

Do you look at piles of laundry and think, "OMG! I have so much I have to get DONE!" And then are you hard on yourself for doing it faster or more efficiently or being behind? Or do you think, "OMG! Look at the abundance of clothing! Look at the fullness of my life and the ever-present reminders of living fully in these clothes!" How about finding gratitude for the ever-present mindfulness practice known as "doing laundry".

Challenge yourself to be simply present in the moment with every aspect of the laundry cycle without making any part of it mean that something is done or not done or needing balance. It just IS. It will always BE.

The key to masterfully living your life with peace and happiness, is to decide that you will live in the story of ENOUGH rather than living in the story of NOT ENOUGH, because honestly it is only a story and only you are telling it. If you can bust yourself even just one small moment at one noticeable time this week for dwelling in a "not enough" story, you will be well along your way down the path of "Embracing Life."

EXERCISES

GET GUMPTION

Do your next round of laundry as if you were in love with every single moment of the process. Imagine explaining to a child how to enjoy (or even win!) the game of laundry.

JOURNAL THIS:

- ◊ What is going on when you are the most relaxed?
- ◊ How do you know you are relaxed?

GET UNPLUGGED

We only have one moment at a time. Living fully expressed happens in each moment. Don't worry about the whole of life, just take care of the present moment. Then everything falls into place by itself.

MEDITATE THIS:

- ◊ I relax my body. I eat in a relaxed way, walk in a relaxed way, listen in a relaxed way.
- ◊ I find fulfillment when I am slow down.

43

What Does it Take to Make Changes Stick?

How many times have you tried to change something that "never changes"? Let's be real. Do people really change? Is it possible to change long-term patterns in your life? The only constant here is that making lasting change after the initial breakthrough is one of the most challenging things you can do in life.

You can have a breakthrough instantly. You can experience big changes right away in many life areas, but it is the commitment and the courage that determine whether the breakthrough will become part of your reality over a long period of time.

We must go deeper and become aware of how much trust and courage we have to face the unknown. Yes, facing change is a big deal, but the fear and overwhelm of leaping into the huge unknown territory of your life is the primary challenge you must face. .

Do you want to change your food, your work, your money or your relationships? You will not succeed if you only focus on will power and effort. You will not succeed if you plan on riding the wave of excitement following your breakthrough. You must bring forth your deeper resources in order to make a genuine lasting change. These resources are within you and you have referred to them over time as your "gut feelings", your inner wisdom, your sense of what feels right, or your higher purpose. These things are easily accessible with a focused intention. These things are what makes changes stick.

The main thing to notice when attempting to make a change, is how much you are clinging to what you are doing out of comfort or familiarity. Letting go of these things is more difficult than we realize. **If you don't anticipate the resistance you will naturally have to making changes, you already are set up for failure.** A moment of breakthrough feels positive and inspiring. Sustaining the plan and action of making the change stick is the key to succeeding.

Why do you have resistance to making lasting change? Because somewhere in your consciousness you think that a part of you is going to die. You think that because it will die, it is a dying process.

Become aware of the dying-off part of making changes so that you won't resist it out of a subconscious fear or uncovered feelings of discomfort.

In other words, welcome the death/rebirth cycle of change and do not sabotage yourself.

Notice how ironic it is to hear your own mind saying, "I know I should change this" exactly as you are doing the behavior or choice that causes you harm! We allow and allow and allow. Instead, you MUST be willing to face your limiting beliefs about change.

Examples of old beliefs replaced by new ones:

OLD: "Change is too hard."

NEW: "Change is where the meaning and purpose of life happens."

OLD: "What if I don't get what I want when I change?"

NEW: "I am as curious about the unknown as I am afraid of it."

OLD: "Change requires too much work."

NEW: "Making changes brings a greater level of power, meaning and purpose."

Now you can change your relationship with change.

Having a breakthrough and seeing an exciting possibility for yourself is inspiring and produces positive energy. Making changes stick can have you feeling messy and on-fire at the same time.

Changing patterns is about releasing stuck energy and emotion which feels sudden and wobbly a lot of the time. You are choosing to live in a way that is free from habits or conventional "boxes" that most people fit into, so meet this with awareness and intention to "make the changes stick."

EXERCISES

GET GUMPTION

Keep a diary for 21 days about the area you want to change or improve in your life. List the qualities you express each day. List the feelings you have each day regarding the change. Be open and honest with yourself, no editing or compromising. On the 21st day, evaluate everything you've written objectively and see if you find a pattern. Once you see the pattern, you can get out of it.

JOURNAL THIS:

- ◊ Are you open to change? What do you love about your comfort zone?
- ◊ What describes your resistance to change?

GET UNPLUGGED

It has often been said that "Change is the Only Constant." Life is continuously evolving, dying and being reborn. All opposites play a part in this endless circle of life. If you latch on to the outer edge of the moving circle you will get dizzy. Move toward the center and relax in the calm. Here you will know that "this too shall pass."

MEDITATE THIS:

◊ I open myself to greater things in my life.
◊ I trust in the changes I am guided to make.

44

The Power of an Easy Going Mood

When we feel easygoing, we might be in the mood to enjoy being with some friends or do something fun. Or we could simply enjoy the more flexible mindset that benefits us in any setting. Take notice that this type of mood is the most conducive to dreaming and planning for the future.

Have you blocked yourself from creative efforts just because you weren't "in the mood?"

Many people stay stuck without ever manifesting their creative ideas because they sabotage themselves with a belief that "creativity only happens if I FEEL it".

It can also be true that amazing things happen in our lives when we pursue our dream or our creative ideas with DISIPLINE. In other words, it is NOT an option to say, "Well, I just don't feel it today" and put your idea or dream on hold. Do it anyway.

We can activate an easygoing mood by setting aside some time to be alone and let your mind engage in the creative process. Imagine your life as you wish it to be, then see your new circumstances in rich detail. As you allow yourself to feel the emotions as if this vision was already real, your feelings should be inspired and ready to support your efforts toward setting solid plans to achieve goals and create the life you desire.

The action you are taking is to allow your mind to dream. Make this a priority, not a back-burner "if I have time" or "if I feel like getting around to it" activity. Engage your mind in your dreams and you automatically activate the creative process.

Here is the top and most simple way to form new and exciting circumstances in our lives: Let your easy-going mood lead you into creative visualizations. Let go of distracting thoughts and simply focus on imagining your life as you wish it to be.

The key is that you begin to express positive energy that is very powerful. This energy is the basis of all physical substance. When you put this cycle into action, and start seeing results (which you absolutely will see) you are activating your belief that anything is possible. Now, your easygoing mindset is the guiding force you can use to create the dreams in your heart today.

Creativity happens at all levels. Maybe you want peace today. Maybe you want a solution to a project this is bogging you down. Maybe you want a breakthrough in a relationship. Maybe you want a new perspective on an area where you are stuck. This is daily living that requires your creative energy.

Activating an easygoing mood does another important thing for you. It is an acknowledgment that there are limitless amounts of ideas and insights that can help you achieve your goals and simply allow them into your consciousness today.

Like any unused talent, your powers of creativity improve with use and experience. Apply your creative energies by looking for the better ways to schedule your time, find opportunities or plan work. Keep in mind that there is always a better way to do things. Get into an easygoing mood and enjoy your creative self!

EXERCISES

GET GUMPTION

Go into a different setting than your normal routine when you sip your morning coffee/tea. (Your backyard, or a park, or a comfortable couch.) Take this time to indulge in an easy-going mood. Imagine who else benefits when you actively do this.

JOURNAL THIS:

- ◊ What happens when I "do it anyway" no matter how I feel?
- ◊ When and where is your best "easy going" expression?

Our spiritual viewpoint is accessible at any time. All that is usually required is to REMEMBER.

GET UNPLUGGED

MEDITATE THIS:

- ◊ I imagine I am the warm radiance of the Sun, with a bright mind, an open heart, an active body and a fiery spirit.
- ◊ I imagine my free spirit, untethered to any of my thoughts or fears.

45

What Makes it Matter?

When your life has meaning, you are happier, feel freer, and enjoy more peace. When you feel down or stuck, your life seems difficult or meaningless. What makes the difference?

In the teachings of Don Juan by Carlos Castaneda, Carlos asks, "What is my right path?" and Don Juan replies, "All paths are the same: they end up in the same place. What is important is to ask yourself, 'Does this path have a heart?' If the answer is 'yes,' then that is the right path for you."

Follow the path of your heart. So far so good. Now let's take responsibility for the meaning we make in our life.

Bronnie Ware, an Australian nurse who cared for patients in the last 12 weeks of their lives recorded her observations in a book called *The Top Five Regrets of the Dying* (2012).

The most common regret of all was, "I wish I'd had the courage to live a life true to myself, not the life others expected of me."

Jackpot. What would you need in order to begin today, living your life with a higher level of meaning? We can draw from these epiphanies by committing to positive actions in the present.

The second regret of "wishing I hadn't worked so much" can be the catalyst for choosing time with your loved ones instead. Choose time for yourself instead. Make this choice a priority over working too hard, and your life will feel like it matters more and more.

Another top regret is, "wishing I'd had the courage to express my feelings." Do you ever suppress your feelings in order to keep peace with others? Would your life matter more if you stopped settling for a mediocre existence? Would your life feel more meaningful if you became who you are truly capable of becoming?

Make it matter by having the courage to express your authentic self.

Consider this regret, "I wish I had stayed in touch with my friends." Can you imagine being at the end of your life and missing your friends? Would your life have more meaning if you gave your friendships the time and effort they deserve? Friends make our life matter. What are two actions you can take this week to energize your friendships?

The fifth regret was the most striking to me. "I wish that I had let myself be happier." Why live your life in a way that keeps you from laughing properly, enjoying some silliness, and giving freely? If you answer that question with honesty you will see your gateway to making your life matter even more. If you are stuck in old patterns or beliefs, you are playing small by default. If you are fearing change you are pretending to others and to yourself that you are content.

Take the direct route to a life with meaning by risking change, grabbing the courage to do it anyway, and prove that happiness is abundantly present in you.

Psychologist Eric Maisel, PhD, suggests that creative people experience depression simply because they are caught up in a struggle to make life seem meaningful to them. I believe we are all creative beings, and I believe we all strive to create meaning in our lives.

When the blues make you feel like "it doesn't matter", can you shift your perspective from depression toward simply needing a healing in the category of meaning.

I like that Maisel's ideas because they illustrate how the process of creating meaning keeps us away from the blues.

Knowing what makes it matter is a personal question. Our answers are unique and individual and the deeper you can go with yourself into these meaning-making ideas, the more happiness, freedom and peace you have available in your life.

EXERCISES

GET GUMPTION

Get naturally creative by falling still. Schedule twenty minutes for thinking and planning. Go to a coffee shop with only blank paper for planning and dreaming it out.

JOURNAL THIS:

- ◊ Where in your life do you need to feel freedom?
- ◊ What attitudes or thoughts do you need to let go of?

GET UNPLUGGED

Your spirit is naturally creative. Creativity is the love for what you have to offer the world. Give your spirit freedom, and you will discover an endless source of new life through your creativity.

MEDITATE THIS:

- ◊ I possess an abundant source of ideas within me.
- ◊ Inhale gratitude, exhale creative energy.

46

To Brag or Not to Brag?

Were you taught that talking about your accomplishments wasn't appropriate? Have you diminished something great because you are afraid of appearing self-absorbed?

Consider that sharing your brags more openly will give others permission to do the same. We need more good news in this world. We need more role models that teach us, "If she can do it, I can do it!" We need more excuses to take a risk or try something different. We need more opportunities for inspiration.

Bragging about ourselves has become a more common practice in today's world. We brag online and through social media to share positive accomplishments as a way to build community or gather fans (or "friends") which slowly shifts us toward allowing more and more "bragging rights".

I am a private person and it is not natural for me to toot my own horn. In my professional life I value positive self-promotion and am always looking for respectable ways to share my wins and my trophies "the right way". Do you notice that you have an easy time of this? Do you need to turn up the volume in your life, or do you need to turn it down?

If you get triggered by others who brag too much, or by others who hide in the shadows, this is a sure indication that the same part of yourself wants to come forward.

The same part of you wants balance. Where can you give yourself permission to be open about sharing your accomplishments?

If you receive a compliment or an acknowledgment, are you able to share it openly with others? Do you judge yourself or make yourself wrong for paying attention to these things because they are "selfish"?? Start to examine your beliefs about bragging and see if you can let go of the ones that are not serving you. Do this work with someone you trust and see if you can find your way to greater confidence and joy in your life.

What if the brags you share are the very thing that inspires someone else to move forward or open up in a way that is new for them? Ask yourself the important question, "Who is telling me that tooting my horn is wrong?" Notice that it's only you. Now you can realize that only you can ask yourself, "Who tells me that tooting my horn is the RIGHT thing to do?" Give yourself permission. Like many issues in our life, it comes down to following your gut feeling and trusting your inner wisdom at the moment to know what serves the most.

Give yourself bragging rights. Create an intention for your bragging rights so that you can be confident in your delivery. If you know that your bragging is based on your intention to serve the highest good for all concerned, your delivery will be genuine. When we come from the heart, we cannot go wrong.

Do you need to release judgment of bragging? What kind of person brags about themselves? If you are hooked into qualities that are negative, you have some work to do around letting go of your shadow or the part of you that sabotages your potential.

You may be asking, how do I know when bragging is too much? When does positive bragging cross the line into a monolog full of ego and grand-standing? Answer: When it comes from fear or when it comes from selfishness.

You can check in with yourself by asking, "Am I sharing this to promote a positive future, or am I sharing this to soothe my ego and alleviate my fears?" It can only be one or the other. There is no in between. Take full responsibility of where you are coming from, and you are well along the path to joy and celebration.

Look for the WHY underneath your desire to brag. Or in my case, my resistance to brag. If you want your contribution to inspire others, go for it! There are countless reasons to justify a positive brag.

In our personal relationships we can use bragging to strengthen and deepen our connections. Being able to share a celebration is a beautiful aspect of relationship. Bragging also gives us an opportunity to acknowledge others who made the brag possible. What if you used your brags as a catalyst for gratitude? There's a powerful approach.

Ask your partner, "Can I brag for a minute?" Notice how expansive it can feel to be received in your full expression of self-acknowledgment. We really do not get to do enough of this in our lives. I invite you to be a catalyst for others and invite bragging this week. Ask someone to share their "5-star Brag" this week. Perhaps that is a great topic for the dinner table with family.

When we can create a safe space to brag in a positive and authentic way, it's easier to do it successfully in the world. What if bragging is really an attractive magnet that draws people toward you and also draws out the best in others?

Have you ever bragged about someone else? Feels pretty good. Have you ever received stood in the presence of another person bragging about you? It was probably a significant experience, and if you place more intention and commitment to developing it, your life will sing louder.

47

Did You Forget You Are a Rock Star?

Often the simplest solution to improving ourselves is to REMEMBER what gives us the ability to do our best. When we face a challenging situation, our options immediately improve when we step back and REMEMBER who we really are and what we really (truly!) are capable of doing.

It's as if the design of being human includes a perpetual capacity to forget ourselves. We forget how strong we are. We forget that we know the answers. We forget that we have everything we need to succeed. We forget that we have access to all the love or connection that fortifies us. We forget that everything always works out. We just forget.

Remembering that you are a rock star is a game-changer.

Being a rock star means that you are outstanding, unique and confident about owning the stage where you give an award-winning lifetime performance every day.

Make it your new habit or new practice. Any time you feel the twinges of self-doubt, can you have a plan in place to remember the confidence or self-esteem that you need in order to express your greatest self?

What if you had an image of your "inner rock star" that you could pull out of your wallet anytime you needed to remember? This could be a photo of a peak moment in your life, or a photo of someone else who reflects the qualities of "rock star" that inspire you. It could be a symbol or image of anything else that brings to mind your feeling of "being a rock star". All you really need is to access that awareness and act from that source within. I encouraged a client to keep an action figure of Wonder Woman in her purse. It's amazing how much improvement she's getting in her business negotiations. Last I heard, she has two new job opportunities!

You don't need to go attend "rock star" school. No need to buy a workshop or CD set. You have the qualities that most represent your rock star self already in you. Describe yourself as a rock star, or in a rock star moment in your life and write down the qualities you notice. Mine are focused, connected and "lit-up". By bringing these qualities to mind I can work on expressing them. I can turn up the volume on the quality of "lit up" or connected. These qualities are already in me. I just need to make room for them to come forward. They are powerful enough to naturally overcome my doubts or moments of insecurity. These qualities naturally cultivate my rock star self.

When you find your qualities, the important step is to activate them. Yes, TAKE ACTION. How can you do or say things this week that demonstrate your rock star qualities? Keep a notebook and tally your results. Wear something that connects you to a particular quality as a reminder to express it. Place a sign or post-it note on your desk area to remind you of the qualities. You will see profound results from actions at this level.

Give the gift of "rock star remembrance" to others. Since we're not on this journey alone, make it a priority to remind others of their rock star performances. Or rock star way of handling something. Giving is receiving. You bring out your rock star when you acknowledge it in others. Share one of your rock star moments. Or better yet, remind someone of theirs.

It's reasonable that we forget our brilliance. The polarity of this life has us bouncing from light to dark, from good to bad, from victim to victorious. The rock star can own the stage and be fully expressed in moments of celebration or fulfillment only by knowing the truth of the opposite. Remember the popular saying, "You can only appreciate true love when you have experienced true sorrow."

Imagine that your inner rock star has a best friend named "Vulnerable". What a powerful partnership. What might their conversation over coffee be like?

I work with my clients to explore ways to express vulnerability in comfortable ways. This is the path to being genuine and authentic. As a rock star, your highest expression will be based on your authenticity and your integrity (commitment to self), so I suggest entertaining an inner dialogue with "Rockie Rock Star" and your vulnerable self. Give it your own name. They can make beautiful music together.

How about being a rock star when it comes to self-care? Are you willing to be at the top of your game AND get an A+ in personal wellness? Ask your rock star self to take charge of your fitness and food commitments. What a great area to handle, and you can enjoy being PROUD of your rock star self.

48

Why Not Give In?

If you give in to something or someone, do you see that as a weakness or a loss? If you give in, are you compromising part of yourself in a negative way? Let's gain some perspective on this topic, so that our lives can flow easier, with less effort and with greater peace as the result.

The idea of seeing the bigger picture is a great start. If we are stuck in a small perspective, it's usually because of a limited part of ourselves that we aren't able to see beyond. When we open our eyes to the bigger picture, it's much easier to see our opportunity to let go of something or stop holding tightly to something that is more negative than positive.

A client of mine was going through a divorce. The day in court where things would become final included a moment where the financial resolve hinged on a small debt that needed to be paid. Each one thought the debt should be paid by the other one. After everything lined up, the judge took a break and my client went out into the hallway with her attorney. They had just learned that she would be the one paying back the debt. She placed huge significance on this one financial aspect, and did not want to give in. Her attorney gave her a hug and asked her, "Do you want to be done with this or do you want to keep trying to win?"

Then it hit her. She saw the bigger picture of FREEDOM. If she can give in to the acceptance of the debt being on her side, she can walk away in celebration that the whole thing is now done, and she is free. She had to ask herself, "Can I give in to the opportunity to be complete?" All she needed was to see the true value of letting go. She realized that "giving in" felt like opening her heart toward herself.

The energy of giving in causes an open space in our awareness so that we can trust in new possibilities that we didn't create from our smaller thinking. Holding something tightly with any level of fear or control involved is a recipe for being stuck and unhappy. In many circumstances this can feel like the most profound challenge or the biggest stretch you can make in your personal development. The prize is that you quickly become masterful and available to enjoy the incredible results in a very short time of practicing this skill.

Giving in can simply mean a re-frame of the entire situation. If you believe that giving in means that you are losing, then you will resist it every time. You will stay stuck in frustration and opposition. If you believe that giving in is a step upward into freedom, ultimate gain, and greater joy, then you will embrace this choice every chance you have.

Look at the definition of "Counter-intuitive". This would describe an approach to something that is contrary to what seems intuitively right or correct. A counter-intuitive approach is one that does not seem likely to be true when assessed using intuition, common sense, or gut feelings.

If you have an option to "give in" try noticing how stuck you are in your belief that there is one correct way to respond. Sometimes the choice to give in can feel counter-intuitive to our ego, or to the part of ourselves that wants to be in control.

I challenge you to open up to the possibility that giving in is truly the high road in most situations. If we are so set in our belief that we have to win or get our way, we are cutting off the chance to gain something even greater or more powerful that the prize we "think" we need to win. Can giving in feel like a powerful gesture? Are you willing to see it as a powerful choice rather than a surrender of your power?

"Why not give in?" What a great question to ask yourself in daily life. It's more about inviting yourself to trust life in a greater way.

The most powerful perspective is about what specifically you are giving into. What if you are giving in to serenity? What if you are giving in to your greater self? What if you are giving in to Love? Make note to yourself how distinct these areas are from your fear-based concerns around giving in. Do you only see that giving in is about diminishing yourself somehow?

Can you catch yourself giving in to your Ego? Giving in to your selfishness? Giving in to your habits or addictions?

Why not give in to your prayer?

Or give in to your inner wisdom? I have witnessed many powerful outcomes that are 100% based on a choice to allow something great to naturally occur rather than to force control.

If you have glimpses of this kind of flow in your life, take it to the next level by acknowledging yourself for giving in every chance you get. Make it a more consistent pattern. The intention to give into something you value consistently opens doors along your path.

49

Do You Have Personal Jet Lag?

Are there situations in your life where you have not caught up with yourself? Jet Lag is resolved when you become fully adjusted to your current "time zone".

If you take a flight to Seattle the flight attendant will say, "Welcome to Seattle, we have arrived at your destination" and you will get off the plane and move on with your day.

What if you were flying all the way from India? And you had a stop in Tokyo along the way? You would be experiencing jet lag. Part of you would still be where you were before, while part of you has already arrived at your destination. Jet Lag requires that you spend some time catching up with yourself. Jet Lag is primarily physical so it's easier to see symptoms and choose how to take care of it.

What if you have personal jet lag in areas of your life? Are there situations where you have not caught up with yourself? What if you are living from a perspective of where you used to be, rather than where you are? What is happening or not happening that keeps you from being fully present?

I love the analogy of personal jet lag because it sets our mind free to choose the present. We know intellectually that living in the past is not a productive choice. We also know it's easy to ignore the signs that we are stuck because it feels familiar or comfortable. Looking for personal jet lag can be an easy approach to set yourself free from being held back, especially when you are not consciously noticing it.

Three questions to reveal personal jet lag:

> 1. Am I exhausted because I'm physically spent in a productive way, or am I overspending my energy on needing to catch up?
> 2. Am I seeing this situation in terms of what it means to me today or am I comparing how something used to be in order to have it make sense?
> 3. Do I want to be free or do I want to justify the past?

Personal jet lag is based on a fear or challenge in our life. I worked with a client who wanted better connections in her blended family. The jet lag was happening because she felt afraid that everything was "wrong" when communication didn't flow evenly among all family members. She felt challenged to bring everyone harmony. I asked her to notice if she is operating from a past viewpoint of how families "should" communicate. I invited her to bring herself current with what is positive about the communication that IS happening, and to see if the current communication can define her satisfaction rather than needing it to be based on a past expectation.

This type of personal jet lag is a culprit to our happiness. All you need to do to access happiness and peace in the moment is to call yourself out by saying, "OH! I need to catch up with myself right here right now!" Jet lag resolved.

The analogy of jet lag helps us to identify places where we are stuck. The best transformation comes from taking small simple steps. Be easy on yourself. Jet lag is just a state that occurs naturally. It requires some extra self-care and some personal awareness. It doesn't mean there is failure or wrongdoing or lack of any kind. No judgment, just a nice opportunity for adjustment.

Fill your week with the sunshine of being current with yourself. Catch up to your greatness. Celebrate every moment when you arrive "home" to your sweet self.

50

Are You Trapped by NOT Wanting Something?

"I don't want to be stuck."

"My goal is to never be in debt again.

"I hope I'm never unhappy again."

The trap of NOT wanting something is easy to fall into. Instead of spending our time thinking about creating a future we DO want, we spend our time contemplating how we are going to avoid all those things we do NOT want. If you are feeling stuck or unfulfilled in your life, or if you have a history of setbacks in your life, this is an especially easy trap to fall into.

How many times do you catch yourself "Not wanting. . . "

What happens loud and clear on an energy level is you have created a picture of you doing or being exactly what it is that you say you "Don't Want." You have generated an image with your thoughts which is held up by the emotions surrounding it. It's completely ironic that you are putting out such a strong image, surrounded by so much energy that is truly out of alignment for where you want to go.

This occurrence is also huge opportunity to master one of the most powerful skills life: to direct your attention where you want it to go. When you understand your 100% responsibility for creating your reality based on the thoughts you choose to have, your life unfolds in amazing ways. The distinction between living this way and living unconsciously is huge. There are no limits to the possibilities you have in your life when you are at choice with your thoughts.

If you are putting out a picture of yourself as a poor, unhappy person (or whatever else you DON'T WANT), your picture is received on an energy level. Energy responds openly and creates the intention it sees and feels from you. The result is, yes, you do create more of being unhappy, more struggling with money, and everything else bundled in.

Start bringing the things you DO WANT into your life.

When you catch yourself expressing a "DON'T WANT", think instead about how you could shift the statement into a positive WANT.

Choose the opposite quality and form a statement about your WANT.

"I don't want to be poor" becomes "I want to be wealthy."

"I don't want to be stuck doing work I hate" becomes "I want to have a fulfilling job I love."

"I don't want to mess this up" becomes "I want to be focused and on top of this."

One of the most common mistakes we make is to think that wanting something enough will make it happen. Wanting alone is just an idea. We need more than the want. We need belief and we need a goal/plan/structure for WHEN.

There is a line from *Alice in Wonderland* where the White Queen says to Alice, "The rule is, jam tomorrow and jam yesterday, but never jam today." This is a great example of a want keeping your future in the "jam tomorrow" category and never letting you eat it today.

To make jam today, see it and feel it as if it is a positive experience right here in the present. See and feel it as if it is happening to you. The energy you put out from doing it this way is felt all around you and it's amazing what starts to respond and show up in your life. This is the first powerful step to having what you WANT in your life. Be with it in the present.

Notice how NOT wanting something actually feels like you are pushing it out into the future. Notice how you physically feel when you stand there and say, "I DON'T Want. . . . (Whatever it is)."

It's almost as if you are in a NON-place. Check in and really feel what's there for you. Typically just the energy of resistance, which is based on fear, which if you wake up to seeing clearly you would never choose for yourself.

Now start noticing how it feels to say what you DO want. Notice that it feels accessible in the present moment. Notice there is not a zone of negativity surrounding you. Make your choices based on the distinction of these feelings. It's truly easy to start focusing on what you DO want rather than what you DON'T want.

Have a fulfilling week focusing on the positive experiences and results you WANT. Spread positive energy by sharing with others about what shows up in your life and in your awareness.

SUMMARY

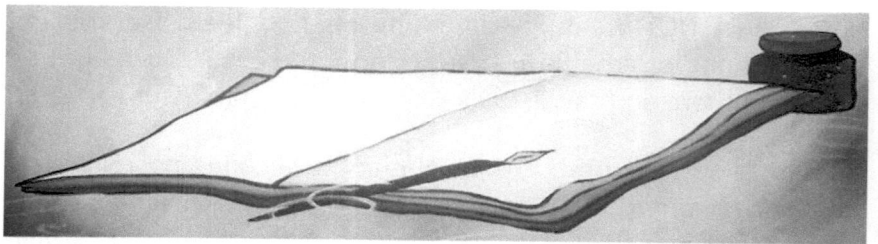

Now that you have experienced this book, I invite you to journal or meditate on each of these statements using your new perspective:

I Visualize the Bigger Picture

I See Things Differently

I Broaden My Horizons

I Lift My Point of View

I Expand My Perspective

Compare your awareness to what you remember at the moment you began the book. Enjoy this journey through your inner landscape.

Acknowledge yourself for your expanded perspective.

Now that you can see things DIFFERENTLY:

> **What you notice that's different in your relationships?**
> **What do you react to in a different way?**
> **Do you pay attention to different things?**
> **Do you make different choices or different decisions?**

Remember this:
Everything is adjustable.

Your perspective creates choice.
Your perspective gives you freedom.

It is up to you to Practice. Choose well. Enjoy.

Take all the time you need to change and improve your life. Enjoy the process of making it how you want it to be.

Own Your Greatest Perspective

"The secret of change is to focus all of your energy, not on fighting the old, but on building the new." -Socrates

Two empowering beliefs about the power of perspective:

My life is influenced by the way I choose to see things.
My perspective changes everything.

Your perspective shows you if you are coming from an empowering place, or if you want to shift into an empowering place.

Your perspective influences your experience in four ways:

What you notice.
What you react to.
What you pay attention to.
What you decide.

When you follow your perspective in any situation,

it will lead you back to your core. Your perspective takes you back into your original beliefs and attitudes. It leads you straight back to where you are coming from.

This isn't an easy task, and it may take a lot of practice to follow your perspective. Make the conscious choice to practice it and soon it will come naturally. Imagine the freedom and joy of being in charge of feeling good all the time!

You must activate your awareness of HOW you choose to see things. Notice where you are standing, and how this influences your view. Notice your position. Your angle. Everything is adjustable.

> **Your perspective creates choice.**
> **Your perspective gives you freedom.**

Record Your Manifestations

Instead of waiting until you reach a goal to be proud of yourself, be present on your journey toward reaching your goal.

Who have you become as a result of pursuing the goal?

Acknowledge yourself, feel the pride, and enjoy the process.

You worked hard to take action and express your gumption. Now reward and acknowledge yourself by tracking your results.

Don't abandon yourself by not designating your successes. Make it official and known when you overcome, achieve and triumph!

Let your milestones be celebrations.

Blocks and Sabotages

Looking ahead to possible road-blocks will make your journey smoother and more enjoyable. You will accelerate your progress by avoiding setbacks or self-sabotage.

Five blocks that sabotage your Fully Expressed Life:

ONE:

Not owning your part in the dance.

TWO:

Not feeling that your future can happen.

THREE:

Being vague, confused or ambivalent about what you want.

FOUR:

Not really believing deep down in your own potential.

FIVE:

Not giving your vision enough time to happen.

The more self-aware you are, the more power you have.

FINAL WORDS

> If you have at least one new tool or one new perspective to use for creating a life you love, I have achieved my heart's desire in writing this book.

Now you can begin and maintain the process of eliminating the inner or outer blocks that keep you from achieving your fully expressed life.

Remember to see the world as your abundant garden. Your joyful work is to plant seeds from Love and water them daily.

- ◊ You must live with intention and take appropriate action.
- ◊ Your GUMPTION is the water for your beautiful garden.
- ◊ Bask in your UNPLUGGED PERSPECTIVE every moment.

It is up to you to be in gratitude for everything the world provides to you, all day, every day.

The more consistent your gratitude, the greater the fields of colorful blooms you see each step of the way.

About Jenifer Novak Landers

Jenifer Novak Landers is a Life Coach who works with individuals and within businesses to facilitate personal growth and fulfillment. She is certified through JFK University and Ford Institute for Integrative Coaching and established Fully Expressed Potential in 2005.

She is an appreciated group facilitator, speaker and workshop leader. Jenifer pulls from her 20 years' experience working in the areas of business development, facilitating business groups and leading women's events and retreats. Jenifer's first successful career was in graphic design, where she became the top sales representative at a major printing company in Southern California. She learned first-hand how creative environments function and thrive, and what it takes for people to be at the top of their game.

Jenifer began her entrepreneurial path when she launched "Novak Art Studio" specializing in residential/commercial murals and children's book illustration for more than fifteen years.

Jenifer is currently developing a line of products called Unpluggables^{TM} — inspired pockets designed to cover smartphones when people choose to unplug for a while.

Jenifer resides in Folsom, California with her teenage daughter, Stella, and a sweet orange cat.

She can be reached via www.fullyexpressedpotential.com or the Unpluggables website at www.unpluggables.com.

Need a Speaker?

Do you know of an organization that would benefit from a presentation based on topics from "Fully Expressed Living?" Jenifer Landers travels from Folsom, California and welcomes opportunities to speak to groups and at events and conferences.

Please email us with information:
jenifer@fullyexpressedpotential.com

Resources

Would you like a printable worksheet featuring the exercises in this book?

Request via email to: jenifer@fullyexpressedpotential.com

Opportunities to Connect:

Schedule a private "Fully Expressed Living" coaching session with Jenifer.

Join our newsletter list for additional perspectives and ongoing motivation to live fully expressed.

Connect with Jenifer on Facebook:
www.facebook.com/fullyexpressedpotential
Email Contact: jenifer@fullyexpressedpotential.com

UNPLUGGABLES™

Discover resources and products to help you choose to unplug from your smartphone.

You can also order a custom design with a quotation from this book for your own personal Unpluggable™.

Visit the website for more information: www.unpluggables.com

Join the "Magic Happens Unplugged" movement and download a free mini-poster.

Acknowledgements

I am in love with so many people for being part of my life and supporting my creativity. I am grateful to share this book with you:

My beloved family, my cherished friends: Because you surround me with love and support that is priceless and true. Because you are there for me always.

My clients: Because you are the reason this book exists. I am grateful for the privilege of sharing the evolution of your life.

My sister, Jo Novak Daley: Because you are the best sister I could ever want or dream of.

My daughter, Stella Landers: Because you are my heart and my everything and I dedicate this book to you and your amazing present and future.

My Life Coach, Debbie Leoni: Because you are my perfect mirror and partner on the path.

My beloved Karl Palachuk: Because without you I would not have finished this book.

My mastermind group: Because you keep me playing a bigger game and reaching higher.

My Woman's Circle "Constellation": Because without you I would not be the woman I celebrate today.

Gratitude and Love.

www.ingramcontent.com/pod-product-compliance
Lightning Source LLC
Chambersburg PA
CBHW021125300426
44113CB00006B/299